CURRENCY CONSPIRACY

Navigating the Global Financial Mirage

Vikram Kumar

CONTENTS

INTRODUCTION

In the labyrinth of global finance, a secretive symphony orchestrates the rhythm of economies, weaving a tapestry of power dynamics that shape the fortunes of nations and the destiny of societies. With whispers of wealth flowing through the hidden corridors of power, a saga unfolds—one of influence, intrigue, and intricate stratagems that unveil the dance of dominance amongst the architects of our economic epoch.

As we embark on this exploratory odyssey through the enigmatic pathways of monetary manifestations, the realms reveal tales of remarkable resilience, cunning conspiracies, and the silent symphonies of the sovereign and the subjugated. Each chapter unwraps layers of lore, from the shadows of the powerful titans to the luminous spirits who strive amidst the tapestry of tales woven by currencies and conquests.

Navigating through historical halls where echoes of the past reverberate with timeless tales, the journey ventures into contemporary canvases where the artistry of influence continues to color the global economic ethos. This odyssey invites a discerning delve into the dynamics that dictate the directions of currencies and cultures, from the influential architects who craft colossal constructs, to the subtle, pervasive impacts that shape societies and souls.

Steeped in the richness of recounted experiences and embroidered with enlightening insights, this tapestry brings forth the vibrant threads of varied visions—providing a panoramic perspective that paints a portrait of the prevailing paradigms and the potent potentials that pulse with promise for the future of our financial frontiers.

In the heart of this book lies a choreography of currencies, where every movement holds meaning, every strategy signifies subtle symphonies, and every note narrates a novel nuance. Welcome, to an enlightening exploration where we decipher the danced dynamics, unravel the unspoken, and illuminate the invisible influences of the mysterious world of money and might.

INTRODUCTION

Evolution of Money

No system perhaps bears as gentle yet firm a touch on our everyday lives as money; a spectral hand guiding us, limiting us, and, in many cases, inspiring us. This curious, invisible power is about to unfold in the ensuing pages, tracing its footprints back to the rudimentary days, meandering through history, and finally looking forward to its imminent future.

Long before the blossom of the internet era allowed for the emergence of cryptocurrencies, long before the world economies were tethered to the sturdy fortitude of gold, human beings found value in seemingly mundane items. Bartering was our first flirtation with the concept of worth. A cow could be exchanged for a couple of tools, or perhaps a bushel of grain. Fairly straightforward, isn't it? However, this system was far from perfect, leading us to our first tryst with standardized money.

The quote by Simon Sinek perfectly encapsulates this shift, "Money was created as a tool to transcend the barter system, to break the restriction of transacting just within our tribes, to enable our lives to expand and our tribes to intermingle". The inception of such a concept opened a new world of possibilities, novel opportunities for human civilizations to burgeon.

Thus began the age of tangible assets like gold and silver, crowned as the physical representations of purchasing power. People now had a consistent measure of value that required no subjective examination. Isn't it interesting to think that at one time these precious metals transformed from ornamental novelties into the lifeblood of bustling markets?

Profoundly, this phase was just one part of the grand evolution of money. Civilizations flourished and fell, technological innovations reshaped societies, and financial systems metamorphosed as a reflection of these dynamic changes. The tangible slowly relinquished its rule to the intangible, setting the stage for a revolution. Welcome to the age of digital currency.

Even though we now live in a world where money is mostly represented by numbers on a screen, the sanctity of the concept hasn't changed. As American Novelist, Ayn Rand, notably said, "Money is only a tool. It will take you wherever you wish, but it will not replace you as the driver." Cryptocurrencies, smart contracts, and tokens may be the newest evolutions in our financial ecosystem, but the essence remains.

In the upcoming pages of this book, we will delve deeper into these transformations, pulling back the curtain on the inherent complexity of our financial systems, and thus, enhancing our understanding of the elusive money trail.

Just as money has journeyed from barter to Bitcoin, our understanding of it is about to embark on a similar voyage. So, buckle up and get ready for the ride as we set sail to navigate through the intricate maze of the global financial mirage.

The Rise of Currencies

In the grand narrative of human history, the development of money is an oft-overlooked saga. Yet, it's rife with fascinating anecdotes and monumental shifts that have indelibly marked the trajectory of societies. Let's learn the whirlwind of historical events and cerebral deliberations that have given birth to national currencies; monetary symbols that epitomize the economic well-being and prosperity of nations.

Our journey begins way back in the seventh century BC in Lydia (modern-day western Turkey) where the first coins as we know them were minted. In an exciting historical twist, the Lydians, known for their ingenuity in business and trade, invented coins as a solution to an insurmountable hurdle – the inefficiency of the barter system. As Herodotus, the Greek historian, hailed, "The Lydians were the first people we know of to use a gold-and-silver coinage and to introduce the retail trade."

The notion of coinage spread like wildfire across continents, reaching the shores of other great civilizations of the Ancient world. The Greeks embraced coins and applied their artistic prowess to craft some of the finest coins history has ever seen. Meanwhile, the Roman Empire, an economic powerhouse in its prime, established the denarius as a standard currency. This solid gold coin enabled trade across the length and breadth of the Empire, stretching from the sun-baked sands of Egypt to the foggy hills of Britannia.

Fast-forwarding centuries later, you'll find that the concept of money took a dramatic turn with the advent of paper notes in China during the Tang Dynasty, saving the arduous trouble of carrying heavy metal coins. Following the footsteps of China, Europe soon embraced this novel idea. Prominent families like the Medicis in Italy issued notes of credit, and thus, the first traces of modern-day banking started to take shape.

As nations were sculpted by the relentless chisel of time, each country began printing its own unique form of paper money, marking the rise of national currencies. This marked the evolution from a unifying measure of trade to a marker of national identity. Each banknote was invested with the soul of the nation it represented, emblazoned with images that were emblematic of the country's values, heroes, and history.

As James Buchan astutely mentioned, "Paper money has had the effect in history of allowing a country to spend more than it seems to earn, with the result that its standard of living and political power have, almost by accident, been inflated."

This account serves as merely the opening chapter in the grand odyssey of currency, a journey fraught with hyperinflations and recessions, monetary policies, and relentless globalization. But at its heart lies the inalienable truth - money, in its limitless forms, is an unparalleled mirror of the economic health and national prosperity of a land, an introspective look into the heart of a nation. Through this book, let us unravel these stories one banknote at a time, one coin at a time.

Historical Highs and Lows

From the bustling markets of ancient Persia to the polished office buildings of Wall Street, history is peppered with fascinating tales of currency's dramatic leaps and plunges. Each shift painted an indelible mark on the canvas of global economics and continues to inform our understanding today. Here we will embark on a riveting journey back in time, unearthing the engrossing tales behind these monetary upheavals.

Money's pulse has always beat in time with the rhythm of our world, becoming a mirror to the political, societal, and technological ebbs and flows of its era. Each high and low in its journey is imbued with a rich tapestry of global narratives that turned mere metal and paper into markers of prosperity or harbingers of doom. Of these tales, few stand out as starkly as the 'Mississippi Bubble' of the early 18th century.

Consider the words of influential economist Adam Smith, "All money is a matter of belief". The Mississippi Bubble was the manifestation of such belief gone awry. French financier John Law convinced desperate investors to funnel capital into his Mississippi Company, touting it as a vast treasure chest of New World wealth. Emboldened by Law's charisma and tactics, investments peaked and pushed French currency to new highs. However, when the facade of anticipated riches crumbled, the shock ripples pushed the French economy into ruin. This cautionary tale underscores the precarious dance between belief and financial reality.

History is, unfortunately, all too familiar with similar tales. Remember Germany after World War I? The harsh stipulations of the Treaty of Versailles imposed crippling reparations on the defeated nation, leading to unprecedented levels of hyperinflation. Money lost its worth so swiftly that workers would rush to spend their wages, fearing the notes would devalue further by evening. An anecdote tells of a woman who left a basket of money outside, only to discover thieves stole the basket and left the money behind. As George Bernard Shaw wisely noted, "If history repeats itself, and the unexpected always happens, how incapable must man be of learning from experience!"

But amidst these tales of monetary follies, there also echo stories of triumph. The remarkable recovery of Japan in the post-WWII era, often referred to as the 'Economic Miracle', saw a devastated country rise from its ashes, revitalizing its currency and becoming a global economic powerhouse. This remarkable turnaround attests to the resilience of economies and adapts the famous quote by Friedrich Nietzsche to fit the fiscal context, "That which does not kill us, makes our economy stronger."

'Money', as Gertrude Stein once said, "is always there, only the pockets change". Raiders of forgotten treasures, students of historical intricacies, and curious wanderers of economic landscapes- lend me your keen ears as we delve deeper into the resonance of currencies with humanity's historical symphony, highlighting their highs and lows while aiming to extract precious insights for our present and future. After all, as we uncover the secrets of yesterday, we only get better equipped to decipher the economic riddles of today and tomorrow. Hold onto your seats as we continue unfolding the captivating saga of our global monetary system.

Modern Money Mechanics

Step right in, dear reader! Don't be shy. We're about to uncover the technicolor tapestry of modern money mechanics - a spectacle that has as much drama, intrigue, and suspense as a Hollywood blockbuster or a carefully crafted detective novel. But fear not, for though the journey may seem convoluted at first, remember the wise words of Maya Angelou, "All knowledge is spendable currency, depending on the market."

Right here in this section, we'll eschew the impenetrable financial jargon, and instead delve headlong into stories, anecdotes, and metaphors to reveal the grand mechanisms of our contemporary financial universe. This narrative is as much a tale about the technology that powers modern money as it is about the people who spend, save, and invest it.

Let's begin our journey in the digital realm, a territory that is likely quite familiar. Each day, we casually toss around the phrase 'digital money' or 'online transactions', but seldom do we pause to reflect upon the quantum leaps in technology and policy that have enabled our everyday conveniences.

Let's rewind just three decades to a time when computers were chunky behemoths confined to offices and ATMs were a novelty. The digital revolution of the 90s, however, forever revolutionized our relationship with money. Online banking took its nascent steps into our lives, turning physical cash into simple numbers displayed on a screen. Pioneers like PayPal pushed the envelope further, allowing us to send and receive money in seconds over the internet. Can you imagine the incredulity of someone from the 1950s looking at this fantastical reality?

A story that often goes untold is of Tobin McDaniel, credited as one of the minds behind Chase's introduction of a mobile banking app in the early 2000s. Tobin faced a sea of skeptics who branded his idea as reckless and premature. He tamed the wave of skepticism by leading the development of a highly successful banking app, cementing his legacy in the annals of modern money mechanics.

Fast forward to today, fintech unicorns, boasting valuations in billions, have surged to the forefront, making digital transactions as commonplace as buying bread from a local store. But this convenience isn't just about ease; it has had far-reaching implications. For scores of people hitherto marginalized by the traditional banking system, digital money has enabled financial inclusivity. Today, a street vendor in Mumbai can receive payments instantly through a mobile app, evidencing a real triumph of financial technology.

But just as we were getting comfortable with digital dollars and online banks, the narrative took another dramatic twist - the birth of Bitcoin. As Robert Kiyosaki, author and successful entrepreneur exclaimed, "Bitcoin is open source money, traditional money is the government's money - that's the biggest difference." Yes, dear reader, the invention of cryptocurrency brought along a fascinating disruption, provoking us to question the very essence of money.

Armed with blockchain technology, cryptocurrencies heralded an era of decentralized money, untethered from the reins of governments and their central banks. The story behind its mysterious creator, Satoshi Nakamoto, remains one of the greatest enigmas of the internet era. Satoshi, through a mere nine-page whitepaper, unleashed a monetary revolution unseen ever before.

Meanwhile, central banks worldwide didn't just idly watch; they're in the early stages of releasing their own digital currencies. The digital Yuan in China stands as a glimmering ode to this monumental shift. It prompts an inevitable clash

– the titans of decentralized cryptocurrencies pitted against the government-backed digital fiats. Buckle up; we're in for a rollercoaster ride!

Our exploration doesn't conclude here. As we tumble further down the rabbit hole, we'll examine the mechanics of global trade, currency exchanges, and the far-reaching implications of national debts and deficits. Remember, "Money moves the world," as affirmed by Sophocles, and essentially, provokingly, notoriously, we are its move-makers.

So, while we navigate this mesmerizing maze of modern money, invite curiosity, challenge the norms, and expect drama – our financial world is nothing short of a stage, and we are all but actors, playing our unique parts. Let's unravel these captivating stories of contemporary financial mechanisms together, one transaction, one bitcoin, one digital dollar at a time!

Conceptualizing Currency Manipulation

"Money - it's a gas," sang Roger Waters of Pink Floyd, and perhaps there has never been a more fitting way to describe the mysterious ebb and flow of international currencies. Just as gas expands to fill any space it's given, money shifts and adjusts to fill the ever-changing landscape of the global marketplace. But the motion of this cash-current can be altered, even manipulated. Welcome, ladies and gentlemen, to the mystifying realm of currency manipulation.

Long a tool in the arsenal of countries wishing to gain a competitive edge, currency manipulation dances to a tune that straddles the line between strategy and deceit. As former Chairman of the Federal Reserve, Alan Greenspan, once said, "Monetary policy is like a lawn mower. You've got to mow on a regular schedule, yet also adjust to changing weather conditions." In this case, 'mowing' looks a lot like countries deliberately tweaking the value of their currency to promote their economic interests. But what does this really entail, and who are the puppet masters in this grand monetary puppetry?

Picture this: it's 1985 and the United States is wrestling with an overvalued dollar that's giving Japanese and European goods a budget-friendly advantage to American consumers. The band of five - US, Japan, Germany, France, and the United Kingdom - congregate in the Plaza Hotel in New York. The result? The Plaza Accord. As per this agreement, the quintet engaged in coordinated currency intervention to depreciate the US dollar against the Yen and the Deutschemark. While this significantly curbed the US trade deficit, it also destabilized the Japanese economy, leading to the infamous 'Lost Decade' of economic stagnation in Japan. An enchanting tale of cause and effect that echoes ominously in the corridors of macroeconomics.

Fast forward a few decades, and we find China under the international scanner for allegedly manipulating the Renminbi. Fears dominated that an undervalued currency was making Chinese goods cheaper for the global market, creating a massive trade surplus for the Asian giant and thus, causing significant friction in international trade relations. The American economist C. Fred Bergsten noted, "Intervention by monetary authorities can be effective, but it is much more so if it confirms or amplifies market trends."

Let's learn the various methodologies employed, like direct intervention in foreign exchange markets, where a country buys or sells foreign currency to tweak the value of its own currency. Plus, cue in aggressive monetary easing, where central banks inject a large amount of money into their economy, aiming to influence the value of their currency.

Does all these sound too complex? Maybe an easy quote by Warren Buffett can help, "Investing is not a game where the guy with the 160 IQ beats the guy with the 130 IQ. What's needed is a sound intellectual framework for decisions." And that's what we will strive to develop here - an intellectual framework to comprehend this not-so-innocuous power play.

Beware of the turbulent whirlpools, beware of the misleading mirages, and buckle up for an exciting sail through the curious straits of currency manipulation. Whether you're a seasoned professional riding the wave of financial trends, a giddy economics student eager to dissect complex concepts, or a curious reader intrigued by the theatrics of the financial world, our journey promises rich rewards.

From the formation of explicit pacts like the Plaza Accord to the hushed whispers accusing countries of currency hoodwinking, the plot is teeming with engrossing narratives. As we explore the uncharted territory of currency manipulation, we'll pick up some tried-and-tested navigational tools, powerful quotes, and memorable wisdom to savour and share. Let's journey together through this labyrinth, one currency plot at a time, as we unfold the fascinating world of currency manipulation.

In the end, it seems, it's really all just a game of Monopoly on a grand scale. As we move our pieces across the board, it's worth remembering the words of Colin Powell, "A dream doesn't become reality through magic; it takes sweat, determination, and hard work." Let this be our motto as we explore the intricate phenomenon that is currency manipulation.

Global Impact and Relevance

Have you ever paused to ponder over the growing relevance, in our interconnected world, of something as mundane as the five dollar bill in your wallet, or the obscure coin buried deep in your briefcase? Much like individual threads in a sophisticated tapestry, these pieces of currency are deceptively viewed as simple and inconsequential, while in fact they are pivotal components in the vast and complex global monetary system. Here we shall attempt to navigate the labyrinthine world of currency manipulation and its consequential impact on the very fabric of global economies, trade, and relations.

Pablo Picasso once said, "Everything you can imagine is real," and this statement is strangely apt when considering currency manipulation. It's an enigmatic game of illusion and mirage, where facts and value can distort and dissolve like a desert mirage. The seemingly solid ground beneath the global economy can shift suddenly due to the tremors of manipulated currency rates, leaving nations and corporations alike struggling to find their footing amid the resultant economic quakes.

Take, for instance, the well-documented case of China's currency manipulation saga in the early 2000s. Sometimes labeled as the "quiet economic war", this phenomenon was not unlike the proverbial iceberg; much of the impact lay unseen, beneath the surface. When China joined the World Trade Organization in 2001, they vowed to let market forces guide the value of their currency, the yuan. However, the reality spoke a different tale as they began artificially devaluing their currency, making their exports cheaper and more attractive. The ripple effects were far-reaching, leading to vast trade imbalances, loss of jobs in other countries, particularly in the manufacturing sector, and strained economic relations.

This incident aptly portrays the domino effect that occurs

when a single piece in the intricate puzzle of global financial markets is meddled with. As the American entrepreneur and author, Robert Kiyosaki rightly stated, "In the world of money and investing, you must learn to control your emotions." In practice, this often proves easier said than done as the artificial manipulation of currencies brews a perfect storm - sparking emotional reactions, influencing politics, and shaking long established socioeconomic structures.

Extrapolating from the past, the future portents the emergence of similar issues in the realm of digital currencies, like Bitcoin...and the dance continues, albeit to a different tune. What was once on solid paper, now exists in volatile bits and bytes. The dance floor may have changed, but the dance of currency, influence, and power remains the same.

So buckle up, dear readers! As we traverse this financial maze, remember the words of Seneca, the Roman Stoic: "He who does not know what the world is, does not know where he is. And he who does not know for what purpose the world exists, does not know who he is, nor what the world is." We're here, trying to know the world, one coin, one note, one byte at a time.

ARCHITECTS OF INFLUENCE

Historical Presence

The Historical Presence section begins with a simple yet powerful assertion: No nation is an island when it comes the global economy or currency values. From ancient civilizations to digital-age economic superpowers, each nation has played a unique role in sculpting the monetary world we now navigate. It's a complex, interconnected tapestry where the warp and weft have been woven by different nations.

So, let's journey through time, space, and monetary values to investigate the fascinating relationships between nations, their currencies, and economic trends. En route, you'll discover the depth and breadth of influence these money maestros have had, and continue to exert, on the global stage.

In the era of kings and empires, gold was the universal currency. An intriguing anecdote here is the story of Mansa Musa, the ancient emperor of Mali, rumored to be the wealthiest individual of the Middle Ages. Musa's legendary Hajj pilgrimage in 1324 left a lasting impression. He spent so much gold on his route that his generosity inadvertently triggered local hyperinflation, devaluing gold for a significant period. Sounds unthinkable, right? Yet this historical moment elucidates a fundamental economic principle: when a nation's wealth (in this case, Mali's gold) significantly influences its currency's value, the world takes notice.

Fast-forward to recent times, and the United States stands as a modern pioneer of monetary influence. A quote from former French President Valery Giscard d'Estaing springs to mind: the US has an "exorbitant privilege" because of the dollar's global dominance. This privilege allows the United States to run large trade deficits without seeming to penalize its economic performance.

But is it really a 'privilege,' or could it become a burden? Economists hold divergent views. Nobel laureate Robert Mundell argues, "Great powers have great currencies." Using their currency clout, the United States has manipulated global money markets to their advantage. However, controversial economist Paul Krugman counters that such dominance makes the US vulnerable to inflows and outflows of capital, causing potential instability.

These expositions, from Mansa Musa to Robert Mundell, reveal the symbiotic relationship between nations, their currency values and global economic trends. Every player on this global stage, past and present, leaves an indelible imprint on this intricate game of power and money.

Here we'll weave more such narratives, exploring the constant ebb and flow of influence and relationships within this complex economic web. On side notes and in margins, we'll pause to reflect on thought-provoking perspectives, challenging the norms as we step together into the uncharted territories of global finance.

So, buckle up: we're about to dive deep into the hidden passages of history that echo in our present-day fiscal dialogues. Here comes the intriguing dance of power, wealth, and the infinite art of money flip.

Political Strategies

As we delve deeper into the complex world of global finance, no exploration would be complete without a look at the potent role political strategies play in molding the value of currencies.

Consider this: when a politician takes the podium, their remarks aren't just a momentous speech for media headlines. It's the hidden force guiding the ebb and flow of the world's money markets. As Sir Winston Churchill once remarked, "Politics is almost as exciting as war, and quite as dangerous. In war, you can be killed once. But in politics, many times." This is the labyrinth we venture into, where a single decision, a careless word, or a strategic move can create ripples across the stock markets, leading to fluctuations in currency values that can alter a nation's economy.

Take, for instance, the historical episode of the Nixon Shock in 1971. President Richard Nixon, addressing the nation, declared an end to the convertibility of the US dollar to gold, effectively placing a giant question mark on the dollar's worth. What followed was a staggering upheaval in the global finance landscape, causing currencies around the world to float freely. This action was a political strategy, designed to address domestic issues such as inflation and unemployment, but one that carried massive global repercussions.

Another enlightening anecdote is the Greek debt crisis. The economic and political decisions of the Eurozone nations played out dramatically, affecting the value of the Euro. The uncertainty injected into the markets by the potential 'Grexit' led to volatility, with ripple effects felt far beyond Europe's borders. Memories of late-night negotiations, political maneuvers, and emergency meetings all served to underline just how interlinked political strategy is with our everyday financial lives.

There's a quote by renowned economist Milton Friedman that beautifully captures this intricate tie. He said, "Inflation is always and everywhere a monetary phenomenon in the sense that it is and can be produced only by a more rapid increase in the quantity of money than in output." The politicians, through their actions, be it economic policies or strategic decisions, often indirectly dictate this "quantity of money".

Let's do a deep dive behind the headlines and bring to attention this interplay between politics and currency. We'll be tracing the whispers of political maneuverings rumbling through the global financial markets and decipher the strategic dance that shapes our financial futures. In doing so, not only will we be removing some of the mirages that mask the realm of global finance but also provide you, the reader, a valuable insight. An understanding which, I believe, will make navigating the global financial landscape a less daunting and a far more engaging endeavor.

Global Dominance

Dawn broke over the bustling city of Tokyo on August 15, 1971. The restless energy that typically characterized this effervescent capital was suddenly seized by an unexpected shiver of uncertainty. The entire financial world shuffled uncomfortably at the declaration that came from the other side of the Pacific. President Richard Nixon had announced that the U.S. dollar was no longer convertible into gold, marking a seismic shift in global economics.

Economist John Maynard Keynes once sagely remarked, "The world is ruled not by intellect, but by influence." And those words were never more potent than in the backdrop of this development. It wasn't just a change of currency policies; it was the dawn of a new era, one in which economic dominance took centre stage in the theatre of global influence.

This momentous decision catapulted the United States into an unprecedented position of power. The US dollar - now disentangled from the glimmer of gold - morphed into the de facto global currency. Anecdotes from Wall Street to the souks of Dubai began to echo the same sentiment - the strength of the dollar was a pulse check on the world's economic health.

In the alluring tapestry of global economics, threads of interdependence weave their own stories. A stark example was evident in the aftermath of the 2008 financial crisis. When the dollar stumbled and interest rates hit rock bottom, economies worldwide buckled at their knees. In a world where every detail is intertwined, fluctuations in the dominant US dollar send ripples across the global financial pond.

We find ourselves in the domain of an intricate ballet, where one dancer's swift pirouette can set off a synchronised ripple effect. The dominant economies, like seasoned ballerinas, navigate the stage with calculated precision. Their role in controlling currency trends is an art that requires years of practice and understanding.

In the words of financial maven Warren Buffett, "Risk comes from not knowing what you're doing." While global dominance in economics can influence currency trends and overall economic health, it also commands a significant responsibility. After all, it's not merely a game of power, but a balance of global interdependence.

As we delve deeper into this engrossing saga, we will examine how dominant economies have leveraged their positions for global influence, manipulated currency trends, and the chain reactions these manoeuvres create. This exploration will be as much a journey into the past as it is a forecast of what the future could hold for global economics.

Pull up a chair, dear reader, for we are about to embark on a riveting journey through the murky corridors of global financial power and the high-stakes game of economic influence. Through tales of triumph, tribulation, and intrigue, we will uncover the secrets of currency conspiracy and global dominance — secrets that power the world as we know it. Buckle up, for every revelation promises to be a twist in the tale!

Policy Impacts

The world is a complicated place, especially when you're in a shirt and tie, sipping coffee, and drafting economic policies that could change the fates of nations and the trajectory of global markets. Let's learn in a nutshell how policy decisions shape national economies and create ripples in the greater ocean of global commerce.

Let me start with an anecdote - the story of the 'Black Wednesday'. It was the 16th of September, 1992 - a day forever etched in the minds of British economists. The British Government was forced to withdraw the Pound Sterling from the European Exchange Rate Mechanism (ERM). Billionaires were made overnight, not the least of whom was George Soros, who made a reported £1 billion by betting against the British policy decision to back its currency. This story is a stark reminder of just how much policy decisions can make or break economic realities.

Now, you might be wondering, "How exactly does all this happen? How do the keyboard strokes of a few policy makers cascade into such significant consequences?"

William Dudley, a renowned American economist, summed it up well when he said: "Policy decisions in isolation can make sense, but the world doesn't operate in isolation." This nugget of wisdom encapsulates the broad reach of national policy decisions, and their tendency to echo far beyond the borders of the founding nation in our increasingly interlinked economic environment.

The impact of policy is often likened to the flutter of a butterfly's wings - a small action that can prompt enormous consequences in our interconnected global economy. Consider the US Federal Reserve's policies around interest rates; a mere suggestion of change sends tremors through Wall Street, impacts the value of the American dollar, and can spell boom or bust for emerging markets half a world away. Policies, like invisible puppeteers, have the power to command financial marionettes on the global stage.

Now let's track policy architects, understand their intent, analyze the outcome, and reflect upon the inconspicuous yet monumental impact these decisions make. From tales of hyperinflation in Zimbabwe to the austerity measures in post-recession Greece, we will journey through the landscapes scarred, revitalized, and forever changed by policy decisions.

So fasten your seat belts; this is going to be a thrilling exploration of cause and effect in policy making and its broad strokes in the economics landscape. Who knows? After this journey, you, too, may come to identify as an architect of influence. Remember as we travel through this journey: "In an era of globalization, your ripple could be someone else's wave."

Future Trends

As we turn the corner into the section aptly titled, 'Future Trends', buckle up for an intriguing rollercoaster ride that will throw a captivating light on the possible future scenarios of global currency manipulation.

The future - permanently elusive, yet persistently approaching – is often a fluid concept. Kenneth Boulding, the renowned economist and systems scientist, once said, "The only thing we know about the future is that it will be different." It's an observation that strikes at the heart of our investigation. The vast landscape of global currency manipulation is no exception to his wise assertion. As we stand on the precipice of radical change powered by digital disruption, globalization, and political shifts, there's a sense of anticipation and decisiveness that accompanies any attempt to decode or predict future trends.

The art of prediction, however, is less a science and more an echo of history. To borrow the words of Mark Twain, "History does not repeat itself, but it does rhyme" - a sentiment that holds true in the realms of global finance and economics. Anecdotal evidence suggests a palpable pattern, a kind of rhythmic regularity that gets overlaid on the diverse chaos of global financial dynamics.

For instance, consider the tale of the US dollar. A key influencer in the architecture of global currency, the dollar weaves an engaging narrative. Post World War II, the US dollar rose to paramountcy, elbowing out the British pound to become the world's reserve currency. In recent years, however, the status quo is experiencing tremors. With China being progressively assertive, unveiling its digital currency, and the Eurozone collectively flexing its financial muscle, we may be on the cusp of a new global monetary order.

In the same vein, the story of the Indian Rupee offers a different vantage point. Once a currency pariah due to its volatility, the Rupee is making inroads into global acceptability, thanks to India's explosion onto the digital scene and a bustling population of young, tech-savvy consumers. It shows that baptism by fire, coupled with a robust approach towards economic reform, can yield noteworthy transitions.

Does this, however, mean that we have the future in our hands? Or are we just mistaking the shadow for the substance? Do these trends suggest a power shift in global currency architectures? In a world that teeters on uncertainty, the answers to these questions are enveloped in both challenge and promise.

Predicting potential future scenarios is much like navigating a maze. As we explore the future trends of currency systems and their prospective architects, let us not forget the words of physicist Niels Bohr: "Prediction is very difficult, especially about the future."

So, hang on tight. This journey promises to be an educative thrill ride riddled with insightful revelations about our ever-evolving financial universe. Strap in, as we continue to navigate this provocative, complex, yet utterly fascinating landscape of global currency manipulation.

Rise of Corporate Influence

In the grand tapestry of finance, there lurks a relatively new and highly influential player - the multinational corporation. Once subservient players to the whims of nations and international bodies, these corporations have metamorphosed into what we might term as the 'Architects of Influence.' Today, it's not merely the global market that thrusts upon these multinationals; they have their fingers on the pulse that directs the rhythm of financial flows. Welcome to the 'Rise of Corporate Influence'.

The narrative of this brave new world begins innocuously. Until a few decades ago, corporations were akin to pawns on the chessboard of global finance, engaged merely following orders rather than giving them. But as national borders began to fade and technology knit countries together like never before, corporations were poised to rise. Suddenly, and perhaps unwittingly, whole nations found themselves dancing to the tunes of these corporations.

Consider the case of the soft-drink giant, Coca-Cola. By the close of the last century, the operating income from its international operations eclipsed those from its domestic front, a rather poignant reflection of the globalizing economy. And with that, so followed the influence. When Coke set up shop in a country, the ebb and flow of the nation's currency value were soon attuned to the corporation's operational tempo. As former CEO Roberto Goizueta once quipped, "A billion hours ago, human life appeared on Earth. A billion minutes ago, Christianity emerged. A billion Coca-Colas ago was yesterday morning." Such is the extent of the reach of these corporations into our life and landscapes.

Or take Apple, a company that, in 2018, saw the valuation of its financial holdings surpass the GDP of two-thirds of the world's countries. When a corporation amasses wealth and resources akin to those of a nation-state, it holds palpable sway over global economic trends and currency values.

As Robert B. Reich, a political economist, and former U.S Secretary of Labor aptly states, "The biggest political change in our lives has been the emergence of corporations and money as the dominant players in politics, displacing citizens and public interest." As these corporations steer the wheel of the global economy, their impact pervades into the lives of ordinary citizens, manifesting in the currency value of their wages, the cost of goods they buy, and even the national policies crafted by their governments.

From the divisions of world powers in earlier centuries to the rise of nation-states in the twentieth, the new world order seems to be governed by the rise of corporations, the architects of an intricate financial mirage.

So, buckle up as we delve deeper, intertwining stories of corporate giants with global economic trends, navigating the murky waters of currency values, and traversing the compelling and complex world of 'Currency Conspiracy.' Remember, for better or worse, we all are passengers aboard this 'financial ghost ship,' directly or indirectly affected by the rising influence of these corporate titans.

Tools of Manipulation

While the soft hum of money minting machines whirs in the background, the puppeteers of our global economy are busy behind the scene, crafting a mirage of fiscal control and stability. This is the pulse-racing world of economic manipulation; an invisible battleground where corporations wield an arsenal of tools to shape currency trends and calibrate the scales of financial balance in their favor.

In this section, we dive into the depths of the rabbit hole, pulling back the shimmering curtain of the global economy to reveal the marionettes and strings driving our economic reality. Like Harry Houdini, corporations perform mind-bending tricks before our very eyes, deceptively altering the fiscal panorama of nations.

Allow me to transport you back to the year 1997. As the Asian Financial Crisis gripped several Asian markets, one corporation stood out from the herd. While others were grappling with depreciating currencies, this corporation was busy implanting itself into the regional economy. As Mark Twain once noted, "The secret of getting ahead is getting started". This corporation, armed with the tools of manipulation, took advantage of the crisis before them, shaping their fiscal reality while others watched in horror.

As we dig deeper into this world of invisible strings and smoke mirrors, we'll tap into the insights of economists, delve into the annals of financial history, and unravel real-life anecdotes. As Aristotle famously said, "The roots of education are bitter, but the fruit is sweet". Our journey might be tough, but it is necessary. Our pursuit is not just the understanding of how corporations manipulate economic trends, but also achieving the skills to navigate through this financial mirage.

These corporations, the architects of influence, no doubt understand the potency of Sun Tzu's words, "All warfare is based on deception". They play their cards close to the chest, tactfully manoeuvring behind the scenes, employing a range of strategies, from interest rate manipulation, currency intervention, and even speculative attacks. But, like all magic tricks, they only work until you know how they're done.

Throughout this chapter, we'll expose the tricks of the trade and the tools wielded by these unseen giants. We'll dissect how they use their influence to shape currency trends and impact global economies. We'll draw back the shadows on the fiscal battlefield to illuminate the maneuvers that underpin our daily lives and wallets.

Buckle up and brace for an enlightening bravura. Welcome to the intricate world of 'Tools of Manipulation'. This is going to be far more thrilling than any Hollywood thriller. By the end, you'll be equipped with the knowledge to navigate your way through the global financial mirage, a skill that is worth way more than its weight in gold.

Sectoral Impacts

In the realm of market supremacy and economic prowess, every industry plays a strategic role - a piece in a vast and intricately structured puzzle that forms the global financial scenario. As one walks down the labyrinthine corridors of this complex edifice, a rising curiosity takes hold. What happens when some of these sectors evolve, devolve or simply, change their course of action? An engaging yet consequential inquiry, and that's exactly where our journey begins in this section.

As a quantative analyst and Investment Banker Oscar Wilde once quipped, "The only thing worse than being talked about is not being talked about." In the context of financial markets, the corporate world's actions influence discussions and debates, shaping more than just market trends; they mold the socio-economic fabric that stretches across continents.

Allow me to narrate an anecdote that will resonate with the theme. In this tale lies the perfect blend of forethought, decision-making, and unprecedented impacts. This story starts in the mid 20th century, with the De Beers Group. A powerhouse in the diamond industry, De Beers had controlled over 90% of the global diamond output, influencing prices and trends at its will. However, in a pivotal move to seek a wider market share, De Beers introduced artificially low prices for diamonds. It was a strategic volley aimed at eliminating competition and solidifying their grip on the industry. But in doing so, they unwittingly catalyzed the global diamond crisis.

De Beers' artificially low prices initiated a domino effect. Africa, an economic ecosystem heavily leaning on diamond mining, suffered severely as livelihoods were disrupted. De Beers' actions had influenced not just their industry but a whole country's socio-economic structure, convincing us unarguably of the power of sectoral impacts.

In a more positive light, consider the innovation-driven tech giants like Google, Amazon, and Apple. Their culture of constant innovation has not only taken their individual sectors by storm but has also reshaped ancillary industries, cities, and even countries. It was Steve Jobs who declared with conviction, "Innovation distinguishes between a leader and a follower." These tech giants, in leading their sector, have altered the face of marketing, advertising, data management, and more, even reinventing cities like San Francisco and Seattle as 'tech hubs' in the process.

In these tales of global empires, we discern the impact of sectoral maneuvers. It becomes abundantly clear that in a world woven together by intricate interactions, the ripples of a single move can traverse far and wide. The potency of actions, whether positive or negative, can shape economies, industries, and societies. This is the realm of 'Sectoral Impacts', an exhilarating journey into the heart of global economic influence. A journey that unravels the power and potential of decision making in the corporate world and its influence over all things large and small. This is our quest – to understand, to interpret, and to navigate the Global Financial Mirage. Welcome aboard!

Navigating Regulations

"Like a skilled captain braving the high seas, slashing through tempestuous waves, the corporations of our time navigate through an ocean of regulations, some helpful, others not so much." Sir Winston Churchill once said, "Difficulties mastered are opportunities won." This quote accurately captures the spirit of corporations acutely harnessing the power of regulations to carve out opportunities where none seem to exist.

Let me tell you a tale that occurred in 2008, an anecdote with global implications that we might term 'The Great Retreat.' Amidst a chaotic financial hurricane, a multinational banking corporation headquartered on Wall Street, playing the role of the beleaguered captain, found itself at the center of an alarming economic storm. With snarling regulations snapping at its heels in its home ground, it sought refuge in the relative calmness of emerging markets. The bank keenly sensed a regulatory arbitrage opportunity that would both shield it from the financial storm back home and allow it to explore new territories.

Now, you might wonder, how does a corporation set sail in such turbulent seas? Well, that's where a role that is seldom talked about comes to the forefront. Enter Compliance Officers, the unsung heroes, the navigators of corporate regulations, leading corporations through the fog of regulatory uncertainties. In our bank story, it was their strategic insight and deep understanding of the subtle nuances of regulation on a global scale that prevented the corporation from capsizing.

But before we delve deeper, let's articulate what regulations truly are – they are societal safeguards, a collection of rules designed to keep our marketplace fair and safe. As the needs of our society evolve, so do regulations. However, in the race for success, corporations often view these dynamic regulations as either a harness limiting their speed or a puzzle hiding opportunities within.

As an extension of this view, a famous quote from Mark Twain comes to mind: "The secret of getting ahead is getting started." Interestingly, to many corporations, understanding the golden word 'compliance' is akin to 'getting started. In dealing with global regulations, corporations find themselves in a complex maze where every corner could lead to a new regulation. But fear not, as navigating through it allows corporations to unlock potential rewards and opportunities.

As we journey further in this section, we will walk the tightrope between corporates' pursuit for profit and the societal need for business disciplines through regulations. From strategies corporations employ to navigate the world of compliance, to regulatory successes and failures, we bring the world of corporate regulatory navigation to you.

If history is any guide, the most successful corporations are those that do not merely survive the regulatory storm but thrive amidst it, rising from the ashes like the mythical Phoenix. The next part of the chapter will present a deep dive into the gritty details of how they do it, peppered of course, with more exciting real-life narratives that illuminate the way. As we unravel this complex world, remember this - rules are not just obstacles to jump; they can also be stepping stones to reach greater heights.

AMERICAN ODYSSEY

USD DYNAMICS

Post War Era

At the heart of an epoch of tremendous change and reformation, the spoils of war had blessed the United States with an economic might never seen before in history, due largely to the ripple effect at the end of World War II. Nation after nation found itself tethering its economic future to the United States Dollar (USD), an economic colossus on the global stage.

In the words of former British Prime Minister, Winston Churchill, "To build may have to be the slow and laborious task of years. To destroy can be the thoughtless act of a single day." These words, spoken in a different context, resonates perfectly with the economic landscape post World War II. What took centuries to build, was shattered within a span of few years, leaving many nations picking up the pieces of their economies. Meanwhile, rising from the ashes was a new global power, the United States, whose currency, the USD, was about to take an unprecedented journey.

Think of it like a game of Monopoly. At the end of a long, drawn-out game, it's often one player who holds all the property cards, with everyone else in financial ruins, or, if they're lucky, clinging on to the lowest denomination bills. Post World War II saw the United States holding virtually all the 'property cards,' and while other nations were busy repairing their war-torn lands, America's economy flourished, and the USD began its meteoric rise to dominance.

Consider the Bretton Woods Agreement of 1944, a relevant and tangible anecdote that underscores the ascent of the USD. In the rural environs of Bretton Woods, New Hampshire, 730 delegates from all 44 Allied nations gathered in the grandeur of Mount Washington Hotel. The objective? To build a new economic order, a new financial architecture that would prevent future wars. The USD, being the strongest currency, was chosen as the world's main reserve currency. From that point on, the fate of global economy nested in the strength of the greenback.

As the great author, Paulo Coelho once said, "Everything that happens once can never happen again. But everything that happens twice will surely happen a third time." The post-war order initially spearheaded by the USD experienced a similar sentiment. Despite several economic crises over the decades, the USD maintained its stronghold, illustrating the resilience and strength that defines its global dominance.

Indeed, the narrative of the post-war era and the subsequent emergence of the USD as a global reserve currency is a tale of survival, strength, and strategic supremacy. As our journey uncovers the hidden dynamics and astounding history of the world's most popular currency, we will articulate the highs, lows, and the extraordinary resilience this iconic currency has repeatedly showcased. This journey, dear reader, is not merely a tale of numbers and dollar bills, but the journey of a nation that monetized its power and the world that hinged upon it.

Nixon Shocks

It started out as a typical Sunday evening. Families were returning from picnics, while choruses of crickets performed in backyards nationwide. Little did they know, they were oblivious to the looming financial shockwave about to ripple through their lives and that of the entire globe. President Nixon was about to announce a dramatic economic policy shift, a day that would become etched in the annals of economic history as "the Nixon shocks."

In the era of Woodstock and moon landings, there was another significant event unfolding that wouldn't grab the public's fascination in quite the same way - but whose effects would be far-reaching and long-lasting. That was when US President Richard Nixon sat before a television camera on August 15, 1971, intending to alter the global economic landscape.

In what economist Barry Eichengreen described as "the most significant monetary-policy decision taken by any President in the post-war period," Nixon declared that the United States would no longer redeem dollars for gold, shattering the post-World War II Bretton Woods system that had maintained global financial stability.

Up until that moment, the global economy was like a well-oiled machine, with every cog - every nation - meshing smoothly together under the Bretton Woods agreement. The US dollar, pegged and backed by gold, served as the fulcrum of this vast and complex mechanism. Abruptly unpegging the dollar from gold was tantamount to yanking a key cog from the machine. The repercussions were inevitable.

In the wake of Nixon's announcement, Americans woke up to a new financial reality. Inflation soared, pushing everyday household items out of reach for many. Yet, amidst the economic chaos, there was also a feeling of liberation. As the economist Milton Friedman observed, "Nixon's bold move freed the USD from its golden shackles, enabling it to chart its own course."

However, Nixon's decision didn't only rock the American economy. Like a stone thrown into a pond, its ripples spread globally, reshaping international economies in diverse ways. Countries tied to the USD found themselves bobbing in a sea of uncertainty. France, for instance, which held substantial reserves in US dollars as a safe bet, found its economic stability suddenly threatened.

Sharing his thoughts on Nixon's policy, famous British economist John Maynard Keynes commented: "When America sneezes, the World catches a cold," markedly encapsulating the magnitude of America's influence on global economies.

Stepping into the labyrinth of Nixon's economic policies, we necessarily embark on an odyssey, navigating through a timescape of upheaval, discovery, and transformation. As we delve deeper into this narrative, we will further examine the repercussions of the Nixon shocks, exploring both dark economic recesses and unexpected streaks of silver lining, all while reminding ourselves that every decision, good or bad, propels us forward on an uncharted voyage of learning.

21st Century Scenario

In Paul A. Volcker's famous words, "A nation's exchange rate is the single most important price in its economy". To answer the mammoth question hovering in our minds about the future of the American dollar, let's take an exhilarating voyage across time, traversing the depth and breadth of its storied past, and into the turbulent seas of its impending future.

Our starting point is the dawn of the new millennium, the birth of the 21st Century, when hope and optimism were as plentiful as the paper dollars being churned out by America's minting machines. Fresh out of the Y2k scare, America had just witnessed the biggest stock market bull run in its history. The tech bubble was inflating, and the Greenback, 'the USD', was unshakeably riding the high tide.

Fast forward ten years, and a notable contradictory scenario reveals itself. The American housing bubble burst, leading to the Great Recession, and, almost overnight, the mighty USD was no longer the global symbol of prosperity. The 'almighty' had fallen to its knees, sending ripples across the world economy. A decade into the new millennium, the axiom, "When America sneezes, the world catches a cold," rang painful truth worldwide.

Now cast your eyes on the present-day scenario – the 21st century is in its adolescence, and we find ourselves in an era where the dominance of the USD is no longer taken for granted. The tide indeed appears to be turning. Cryptocurrencies are knocking at the door, other powerful economies are wrestling for the spotlight, and trade wars are shaking the economic landscape. The question now is, will history repeat itself, or will the USD find a way to regain its lost glory?

Predicting the future is much like predicting weather patterns. Some say it's all in the trends, others argue it's far too random, but in the world of currency, a wise man might say it's about reading the signs. As Warren Buffett insightfully stated, "I never attempt to make money on the stock market. I buy on the assumption that they could close the market the next day and not reopen it for five years." The same can be said about predicting the future of the USD. The signs are all there, reflection upon them can shape our understanding.

Stepping into the next part of this odyssey, we'll delve into key events and trends that have shaped the course of the USD, employing our rear-view mirror to predict what lies ahead. Buckle up as we navigate the monetary mysteries of our time, forecasting the fate of the USD in an uncharted economic landscape, providing you with the knowledge to weather any economic storm thrown your way. Look out for the signs dear reader, and remember, as the great George Bernard Shaw wisely noted, "If history repeats itself, and the unexpected always happens, how incapable must Man be of learning from experience!"

Political Decisions and Impacts

In the grand scheme of the global economy, political decisions often ripple further than the borders of the nations from which they originate. The entangled web of international finance and politics means that a gust of policy change in Washington D.C. can send waves crashing on distant financial shores. Such is the profound influence of political decisions on the value of the United States Dollar (USD) and, ultimately, the world's economic health.

Now, allow me to introduce you to a character central to our narrative. Meet the USD, the shy unassuming money note that, in many respects, holds the world economy in its reluctant grasp.

Most people see the dollar as a tool for buying a burger or a brand-new car. But behind the scenes, that green paper has an intriguing story that's as much about global power and influence as it is about commerce. As James Rickards, a renowned American lawyer and financial commentator noted, "Currency wars are one of the most destructive and feared outcomes in international economics."

One such riveting tale features Nixon's Shock in 1971. It was a regular Sunday evening when President Richard Nixon made a decision that would entirely shift the global financial landscape. By unilaterally cancelling the direct international convertibility of the USD to gold, Nixon sent the financial markets spiraling into the unknown. Thus, began the era of fiat currencies.

In the aftermath, the impact was two-fold. On one side, countries bound by trade links to the USD experienced major economic shakeups. On the other, Nixon's decision played a significant role in pushing the USD to become the world's reserve currency, cementing America's place at the epicenter of the world economy.

Then there's the tale of the Bartender and his Buck. Amid the 2008 financial crisis, a humble New York bartender named Alessandro noticed a peculiar phenomenon. While previously, Italian and French tourists would generously tip, their euros suddenly seemed to hold a tighter grip. It was their reaction to the struggling euro in the face of a steady dollar, a direct consequence of the deliberate moves made by the United States' Federal Reserve, aiming to provide stability in uncertain times.

As it stands, the USD occupies a pivotal stance in the global financial system, impacted by the ebb and flow of political decisions not just on Capitol Hill but worldwide. Thus, navigating this 'Currency Conspiracy' requires us to understand that "Money is politics in another form," as said by economist Duncan Foley.

To grasp the whole scope of our global financial mirage, we need to delve into these fascinating tales of political power moves, unravel the cascading impacts, and comprehend the part played by that simple, unassuming tool of trade – the United States Dollar. Hold tight for this insightful voyage into the intriguing world of international finance.

Public Perspective

Engage in any conversation today about the state of the economy, and you'll find opinions are as diverse as American quilts. Some folks are optimistic and believe we're on a brisk walk towards continual prosperity, while others see an ominous gathering of clouds on the horizon, predicting an imminent financial meltdown. However, the true influence of these opinions extends far beyond mere dinner table discussion. They shape economic policies that in turn govern the throbbing financial heart of our society - currency value.

In this journey, we're going to unpack this complex quilt and explore how public perspectives influence economic policies and currency values. Buckle up and brace yourself for a fascinating ride through the intricacies of public sentiment and their ripple effects on the world of finance. As former Federal Reserve Chairman Alan Greenspan once said, "The fate of the economy is, to a large degree, directly reliant on public sentiment."

Remember the fierce debates in households across America when smartphone apps like Venmo and Cash App swiftly altered traditional financial interactions? There's an insightful story here about how public opinion shaped innovation. Initially, these apps were met with widespread skepticism due to concerns about security and ease of use. The appeal of instant transactions between friends and businesses, however, soon tipped the scales of public opinion in their favor. This shift in sentiment led to a swelling user base, prompting traditional banks to introduce similar features, leading to what can be seen as a 'financial app revolution'. Imagine, such substantial transformation in traditional banking—orchestrated by everyday conversations!

Financial experts would remember the infamous 'Black Monday' in 1987, when the U.S. stock market underwent a seismic shock, plunging over 20% in a single day! It wasn't a real economy crisis, but the chilling fear of impending doom had people pulling money from the stock market, causing a crash. As world-renowned economist John Maynard Keynes once said, "The market can stay irrational longer than you can stay solvent." So, here's the thing: it wasn't the economy, but public opinion driving the market, a fact that echoes the crucial role public sentiment plays in the economy.

We invite you to navigate deeper into public opinion impact stories, making sense of capricious markets, and learning how to ride these waves by prognosticating shifts in public sentiment. Grab some popcorn, because nothing on cable can beat the high-octane drama that unfolds in the realm of finance, especially when public perspectives are the playmakers. And remember, as the American Poet Edgar Guest quipped, "Public sentiment is everything. With public sentiment, nothing can fail. Without it, nothing can succeed."

So, as we embark on this enlightening odyssey through the public opinion juggernaut, we'll challenge misconceptions, unlock insights, and hopefully, come out the other side with a newfound understanding of the financial world we live in. These pages will guide you into the labyrinth of the collective mind of society, equipping you with wisdom gleaned from the past and tools to navigate the future. The journey you're about to embark on promises insights and intrigue in equal measure. So, are you ready to set sail on this journey? It's time we braved the storm, and plotted a course towards a more informed future, whispered in the rustling leaves of public opinion.

SOCIETAL IMPACTS

Main Street vs Wall Street

If Wall Street and Main Street could talk, they'd tell two very different stories about the land called America. Reflecting on this, the renowned American economist, Paul Samuelson, once remarked, "Economics is a choice between alternatives all the time. Those are the trade-offs." Herein lies the tale of two Americas, one basking in the neon lights of skyscrapers, while the other resonates to the rhythm of mom and pop stores.

Let's take a little stroll down Main Street. Here, life swims in the entreprise of small businesses. The coffee from the muted gold pot at Sarah's diner is always hot, flavored with dreams feeding the local economy. Ruby, at her boutique store, lines up hand-knit sweaters. Her crafts echo the resilience of the middle class, riding the tides of economic policy shifts, manifesting silent resilience against market tectonics.

Yet, switch channels to Wall Street, and the frame changes rather dramatically. High-rise buildings pierce the sky, shimmering with the dazzle of high-stake deals, watched over by golden bull itself, symbolizing the wealth and power, deeply rooted in speculative dealings and financial wizardry that seems quite foreign to the residents of Main Street.

Here, masters of the universe gamble on global currency markets, fuelled by economic policies that often dance to the tune of Wall Street's symphony, while Main Street hums a bluesy hymn, dealing with the residual echoes of those policies. A trenchant narrative that swirls around this dichotomy is an instance from the 2008 Financial Crisis—Wall Street's missteps led to Main Street's misery.

Author John Steinbeck once wrote, "Power does not corrupt. Fear corrupts... perhaps the fear of a loss of power." This describes the underlying conflict well. Wall Street thrives on the flow of money and power, while Main Street battles against the fear of its absence, amplifying the effect of the same economic policies through two very different lenses.

My dear reader, as we unravel these very different tales of our society in the pages to follow, I urge you to remember that each Street adds a unique thread to the vibrant American tapestry. As divergent as they may seem, they make a whole. Every silent sigh of a store-owner closing his shop early, every cheer in the trading floor at the close of a profitable trade – these are the harmonies and dissonances in the melody of economic progress that is the American odyssey.

Plunge ahead, and let's discover how this contrast teaches us about resilience, fortitude, and the intricate dance of economic policies. As we traverse this tale of two streets, remember the connectedness between 'wealth' and 'well-being,' Wall Street and Main Street, the ballet of money that keeps the American dream alive and thriving.

Employment and Economy

One of the most vivid memories I have from my early years is of my father, a sturdy clockmaker in our tiny town, often repeating a quirky saying that never made much sense to me then: "Son, remember, even a broken clock is right twice a day." Decades later, standing at the epicenter of the spiraling world economy, the real weight of those words peels back the layers of mystery for me. On many occasions, our global financial system seems just like that broken clock, momentarily aligning with reality, only to spiral away again.

In this odyssey through the intricacies of the American financial terrain, we find ourselves under the subparagraph 'Employment and Economy', a journey through a unique quandary. How does the relentless ebb and flow of currency values and the labyrinth of economic policies affect our everyday employment and the sectors we depend on? Does the dollar rise signify the wellbeing of a worker in Detroit or the prosperity of a farmer in Iowa?

We begin our exploration by throwing light on an anecdote from the era of the Great Depression, a time that still leaves an indelible imprint on America's economic consciousness. Picture a typical American family, the Johnsons, in the year 1933. Mr. Johnson lost his job as the local factory shut down, a direct impact of the depreciating dollar and stringent economic policies following the infamous Stock Market Crash of 1929.

Fast forward to the 21st century, and we find ourselves facing a similar recipe for disaster in the form of a global pandemic. It sets the stage for a comprehensive examination and a sobering comparison of past and contemporary economic times. Will the Johnsons of today weather the storm with more resilience or less?

Few would argue with the assertion of Joseph Stiglitz, a Nobel laureate in Economics, who said, "Creating a learning society is not only an economic necessity; it is also a prerequisite to increased societal well-being." The wave of the world today is growth propelled by knowledge. As such, understanding the strings that connect world currency, economy, and employment become an essential tool for survival.

We will journey together through this multifaceted landscape, exploring the impact of economic measures on both classic and emerging employment sectors. We will decipher the hidden language of numbers and unwrap these complex relationships that dictate the course of our lives. It's time to comprehend the world beyond the formal jargon of economists and financial experts. Because the hidden patterns of the economy affects us all - from the office halls of Wall Street to the serene farmlands of the Midwest. It's time to navigate the 'Currency Conspiracy.'

In the words of noted economist John Maynard Keynes, "The difficulty lies not so much in developing new ideas as in escaping from old ones." So, let's abandon our preconceived notions and embark on a new journey towards financial understanding, for as we navigate through the global financial mirages, we are not just observers but participants, completing our part of the American Odyssey.

Stay tuned as we turn the pages revealing the chapters of modern-day financial paradoxes, echoing the sound truth of my father's words, "Even a broken clock is right twice a day."

Because at the end of it all, isn't the financial world, particularly the world economy, very much like a broken clock too?

Business Perspectives

The pages of this segment are packed with extraordinary chronicles detailing how entrepreneurs, from the mom-and-pop store owners to the CEOs of multinationals, have sailed through the currents of economic trends. These stories are not far removed from Shakespeare's aphorism painted across the pages of 'The Tempest', "What's past is prologue" - for the tales of businesses that have combat economic upheavals unarguably lay groundwork for the strategies of enterprises yet to come.

Whether it's Starbucks evolving its strategy post the 2008 crunch, Amazon penetrating untouched markets despite the financial turmoil, or Kodak's struggle in failing to transition during the age of digital photography, each narrative serves as a testament to the business acumen, foresight, and sometimes the lack thereof, in the ebb and flow of industry trends set to the backdrop of economic tides.

The story of Arthur Blank, co-founder of The Home Depot, serves as an apt anecdote. Following the 2008 recession, rather than hunkering down in a defensive mode, he defied the odds and reinvented his business strategy. He emphasized on customer service, nurturing a culture of respect and care for employees, which ultimately fueled the company's growth through word-of-mouth marketing. Arthur Blank's risky gambit is a shining example of Mark Twain's sentiment, "There are few things harder to put up with than the annoyance of a good example."

In an economy that runs on dizzying uncertainty, businesses have no cookie-cutter solutions to flourish. But by observing the triumphs and tribulations of companies that have weathered these storms, they can glean precious insights to respond wisely to evolving economic trends.

In 'Business Perspectives', we delve into the heart of these narratives, for as French novelist Marcel Proust mused, "The real voyage of discovery consists not in seeking new landscapes, but in having new eyes." Whether you are a budding entrepreneur, seasoned business magnate, or an eager student of finance, this chapter will challenge your preconception of the delicate interplay between business and economy, equipping you with 'new eyes', offering a fresh, informed perspective on economic navigation.

Read on, and let's embark upon this journey of discovery together, navigating the global financial mirage with the oars of acquired wisdom, vision, and bravura from the businesses that were brave enough to weather the storm.

In the end, it is as Peter Lynch says so eloquently, "Believe in something: The natural state of the stock market is to go up. To make money, you must have the courage to get through hard times." It is in our hopes, that this exploration of business perspectives would arm you with the courage to face any economic tempest that may come your way.

Everyday Americans

The hidden hand of the global financial sector often exerts dramatic influence over what we can buy, how we live, and what occupies our dreams—all without us even realizing. This pervasive influence, sometimes subtle and at other times brutally overt, is primarily exerted through the value of our currency and the sweeping economic policies that shape its ebbs and flows. As renowned economist John Maynard Keynes astutely observed, "The ideas of economists and political philosophers, both when they are right and when they are wrong, are more powerful than is commonly understood."

To understand the effects of economic policies on everyday Americans, let's delve into the story of Jane and John Stevens. High school sweethearts from the small, rustbelt town of Smithville, the couple worked faithfully at the local aluminum factory for over twenty years. They believed in the American dream: hard work begets decent wages, which would lead to a comfortable life.

But in 2007, the U.S experienced a recession. In an attempt to stimulate the economy, the Government implemented policies, leading to inflation and depreciating the value of the American Dollar. Recalling a conversation over a humble dinner, Jane noted, "It seems like our paycheck buys less and less every month. The price of bread, milk, everything has gone up."

Jane and John felt the direct impact of expansive economic policy and a shifting currency value. Like millions of other everyday Americans, their life was dictated by decisions made in legislative offices and corporate boardrooms miles away from their hometown.

Not every story is like Jane and John's, of course. Take the Nicholson family from Silicon Valley—as the dollar weakened, the demand for their tech-based export business skyrocketed.

Their prospects improved dramatically as foreign customers found American products more affordable. As Nick Nicholson observed, "An economy is like a pendulum; it swings in both directions, benefiting different segments with each motion."

In the words of Robert Frost, "In three words I can sum up everything I've learned about life: it goes on." Despite the ups and downs driven by macroeconomic forces, everyday Americans like Jane, John, and the Nicholsons adapt and persevere. As these stories illustrate, economic policies and currency fluctuations aren't abstract concepts discussed in boardrooms or economics classes; they play out in the daily struggles and successes of individuals.

Navigating the global financial mirage can feel like steering a ship in a tempest, but understanding the mechanics of currency value and economic policy is the first step towards securing stable ground. It empowers us to mitigate the risks and seize the potential benefits that economic tides may bring.

Everyday Americans aren't just passive participants in this cosmic financial theater. They are the real, living embodiment of economic phenomena, resilient figures that continue to chase the oft elusive but inherently captivating American dream—a testament to the human spirit's undying resilience amidst the complex and ever-changing global financial landscape.

ASIA'S FINANCIAL FOOTHOLD

China's Yuan Policy

Let's take a trip to China for a moment. Clock ticks over to 5.00 am - ponds gasp awake, and the dawn chorus witnesses fishermen casting their first nets. Meanwhile, in a steel-and-glass fortress in Beijing, another net is being cast wider and farther – that of China's economic influence. This economic superpower garners power, primarily through the threads of its currency: the Yuan. It's a tale of clashing titans, global economies caught in the ebb and flow, and the weight of every decision echoing across the continents.

From the mythical land of dragons, China has transformed into a resolute steel dragon, forging new financial paths with its scheduling of the USD-Yuan exchange rates – an elusively complex policy made notorious by the term 'currency manipulation'. As renowned economist Paul Krugman puts it, "Economic policy is a matter of balance, but it's also a matter of power."

China's unique strategy of managing its currency not only raises eyebrows but also incites countless debates, often filled with concoctions brewed from suspicion, fear, uncertainty, and awe. You see, it all started back in 1994 when China undertook a significant reform and pegged its currency to the dollar. This decision, made quietly amidst the dawn of the digital revolution, would have the impact of a phoenix rising from its ashes.

Imagine a high-stakes poker game where the Yuan is China's trump card. A story unfolds from beneath the velvety darkness of opaque policies, where China coolly plays its hand close to its chest. All the while, the world economy, like spectators around a roulette wheel, watches carefully, their own fortunes tethered to the defiant roll of the Yuan.

A vivid anecdote from the time of the 2008 financial crisis

springs to mind. While economies worldwide faltered, China's approach to its Yuan policy held surprising stability. In response to the crisis, China pegged its currency to the dollar, thereby ensuring that as the dollar strengthened, so did the Yuan. This strategy was a buoy amidst turbulent waters, helping China maintain control amid global financial upheaval. The lesson? In the words of George Soros, "Markets are constantly in a state of uncertainty and flux, and money is made by discounting the obvious and betting on the unexpected."

Yet, the implications of China's currency policies reach far beyond its workshops and immense skyscrapers. The ripple effects of the Yuan policy can be felt in the electronics we purchase, the vehicles we drive or, for that matter, the cup of Chinese tea we savor across continents. The game China plays with its currency policy affects us all.

With the Yuan as its sword and shield, China navigates the chessboard of global economics. It's an exciting journey, filled with intriguing tales that demand to be shared. Let's embark on this narrative voyage and see how deep the rabbit hole goes when it comes to China's Yuan policy.

From the tales of the local fisherman to the towering skyscrapers in Beijing, the threads of the Yuan bind China's story together... a story that the world, while sometimes wary, cannot ignore. To quote the legendary Sun Tzu from 'The Art of War', "Know yourself, know your enemy, and you shall win a hundred battles without loss." Perhaps, in understanding the Yuan and its wielders, we can not only navigate but thrive amidst the intriguing mirage of the global financial landscape.

Japan's Yen Journey

In the bustling streets of Tokyo, amidst the blend of historical architecture and modern skyscrapers, a unique saga unfolds - the ever-evolving story of the Japanese yen. Like Mount Fuji, weathering the wrath of the winds and standing resolute throughout centuries, Japan's economic currency, the yen, echoes a similar tale. Its journey carves the path of the nation's economic history and reflects the ebbs and flows of its place in the global financial mirage.

The Japanese word for yen, 'Round', emerged from Spanish silver dollars widely used in Asia during the 16th and 19th centuries. The yen has journeyed from the shadows of the silver dollars to stand as one of the most traded currencies in the present day global forex markets. Amusing, isn't it? That's the yen for you - resilient, surprising yet reliable.

In the heart of the 'Land of the Rising Sun,' the introduction of the yen in 1871 marked the dawn of a new era. Japanese authorities were driven by an insatiable ambition of realizing a unified, modern state. In their quest, they turned to the West. They adopted the principles of the gold standard system, a leaf they borrowed from the European book of economic integration.

"The first step towards change is awareness", noted American psychologist Nathaniel Branden. His words ring especially true in Japan's yen journey. Over time, Japanese people became increasingly aware of the yen's significance, not just as a medium of exchange, but as a narrative of their national identity and global economic posture.

Post-World War II, Japan was devastated and saddled with a crumbling economy. In this ruin, many feared the yen would disappear. Yet, defying the odds, here enters the legendary phoenix of oriental folklore, inspiring the rise of the yen from the ashes of destruction. A series of bold and innovative economic reforms, famously known as the 'Dodge Line' policies, partnered with a buoyant global economy, lifted Japan from the trenches into a full-blown economic miracle.

The 1973 oil crisis, however, burst the Japanese economic bubble. As Japan grappled with the sudden shift in the economic tides, the yen, steady as a rock, shone through the darkness as the beacon of solace and stability. Coined as the 'Endaka' or the high-yen era, this period highlights yen's indomitable spirit. American investor Warren Buffet's quote, "Only when the tide goes out do you discover who's been swimming naked," indeed took on a new meaning in Japan. Despite the maelstrom of challenges, the yen held its ground, reflecting the grit and tenacity much attributable to the Japanese ethos itself.

As we delve deeper into the yen's journey, we uncover not only a currency's voyage but also a nation's metamorphosis. From the ashes of war, Japan rose to become an economic powerhouse, and in its heart, the yen ticked, embodying the pulse of its economic life.

In the second millennium, the yen continues its rollercoaster ride. With a recession, deflation, and now, a pandemic, the yen has braved it all. Today, the resilience of the yen has not only made it a currency to reckon with but also a significant influencer in the global financial arena.

We embark on this eye-opening journey through the dynamic landscapes traced by the yen, learning valuable lessons about resilience, innovation, and the imperativeness of adaptability in ever-shifting global economies. The tale of the yen is more than just a chronicle of a currency. It is, indeed, a testament to Japan's relentless spirit and an unstoppable quest for excellence.

Emerging Economies

The story of the World Economy has been a gripping narrative of constant flux, with the rise and fall of great economic powers. But rarely have we seen such dramatic, nearly cinematic plot twists as we do today. The spotlight is on a part of the world that has long been the abiding muse of countless poets, philosophers, and historians alike. A region rich in culture and heritage, basked in age-old wisdom and teeming with young ambitions - Asia. Under the overarching rubric of 'Emerging Economies', we are going to navigate the labyrinth of Asia's Financial Foothold, the phenomenon creating ripples in the placid waters of the global financial milieu.

To borrow the words of economist E.F. Schumacher, "Any intelligent fool can make things bigger, more complex, and more violent. It takes a touch of genius — and a lot of courage to move in the opposite direction." Asia, with its blooming economies, has given the world that touch of genius.

Let's take a pleasant little detour to China. It's the year 1978, and a spark of economic reform under Deng Xiaoping is about to ignite a prairie fire. Decades later, the smoke has lifted to reveal what many consider a near-miraculous metamorphosis: China, from being a struggling economy, has now donned the mantle of the world's second-largest powerhouse. The ripple in the pond has become a wave.

But the narrative doesn't stop there. It's a relay race, and the baton has been firmly passed to other emerging Asian economies. India, for instance, began its economic liberalization in 1991 out of compulsion, standing on the brink of bankruptcy. Today, it's a Fintech haven and holds the baton with pride as one of the fastest-growing economies.

Swinging down the economic jungle vines, we land in Southeast

Asia. Here, economies like Vietnam and Indonesia offer us a high-stakes drama of aspiration, struggles, and extraordinary leapfrog development. Their story is not one of imitating the West but one of creating their unique version of an economic success narrative.

In the words of the late Singaporean Prime Minister Lee Kuan Yew, "I do not believe that democracy necessarily leads to development. I believe that what a country needs to develop is discipline more than democracy." The Asian economic rise resonates strongly with this ethos.

So, dear reader, time to get your explorer's hat on, fasten your seatbelts and prepare for a deep dive into the erratic yet enthralling world of Asia's Emerging Economies. This exploration may not be an easy one, but when has decoding a global financial conspiracy ever been? By the end of the journey, perhaps we will have a clearer view of where Mama Asia is chaperoning the world economy next.

And as the insightful Paulo Coelho famously penned, "The only thing that traveling requires is courage." In our case, the courage to comprehend the sprawling canvas of global economics. Now, shall we begin?

Regional Competitions

Now we venture into the vibrant and bustling economic landscapes of Asia. Home to many growing economic powerhouses, Asia is a battlefield of financial strategies, intricate negotiations, and competitive behaviors, each nation vying for a leadership spot in the global market.

Imagine the region like an elaborate chessboard, with each Asian nation as a unique piece, each with its attributes, strategic advantages, and vulnerabilities. They are doing their best to navigate the complex, and sometimes treacherous waters of global economics.

One compelling anecdote involves China and Japan, Asia's elephantine economies. Pierce the history of their financial rivalry, and you'd find it colored with tension and startling moves. A notable memory stretches back to 2010 when China overtook Japan as the world's second-largest economy. This dramatic shift, the culmination of China's aggressive growth strategy, signaled a significant shift in Asia's economic equilibrium, disturbing the pre-established order.

Yet, amid the competition, there lies an underpinning spirit of cooperation. As rightly put by John F. Kennedy, "Geography has made us neighbors. History has made us friends. Economics has made us partners. And necessity has made us allies." Japan and China, despite their rivalry, are also each other's major trade partners. Their mutual symbiosis, shaped by need and opportunity, reflects the complex dynamics of regional competition and cooperation.

The narrative becomes all the more intriguing when you add India, South Korea, and the rapidly growing ASEAN economies into the mix. The same pattern of competition and cooperation repeats, illuminating the intricate web that constitutes Asia's financial landscape.

We'll journey through stories of trade wars and economic alliances, currency tussles, and diplomatic tightropes, all under the umbrella of regional competition. Each tale offers a unique vantage point into the bustling economic bazaar of Asia, and the immense global impacts it shapes.

As the acclaimed US investor Warren Buffet once said, "Games are won by players who focus on the playing field—not by those whose eyes are glued to the scoreboard." In the following pages, let us turn our gaze from the scoreboard of national economies to the playing field of regional dynamics, where the real strategies unfold.

The world of Asian economic competition is not just a saga of numbers and growth rates. It's a complex narrative of ambitions and fears, innovation and tradition, conflict and cooperation. Let's delve into this intriguing narrative, decoding the games nations play in the stunning backdrop of the Asian economic landscape. The game is afoot. Are you ready to play?

Next time you skim through economic headlines in the morning, you'll see them not just as isolated pieces of information but as part of an intricate financial dance choreographed on the Asian continent. Let the reading journey that lies ahead make those headlines come alive in a new light. Enjoy the ride, dear reader, as the story unfolds.

Public Response

As we explore the intricate world of international finance, it is imperative to remember the age-old adage coined by Thomas Carlyle, "Economics is a dismal science." Here we aim to unravel the complex skein of economic policies, and their far-reaching influences in shaping Asia's economic history.

Imagine being a fisherman in a coastal village in Thailand. One day, you wake up to the government announcing that the local currency, the Thai Baht, has been floated. Indifferent at first, as weeks pass, you notice your grocery bills mounting, the cost of fuel skyrocketing, and the local school fees for your children becoming unaffordable. This is not a hypothetical scenario, but a snapshot from the terrifying financial crisis of 1997 often referred to as the 'Asia Financial Crisis.'

The collective reactions of millions of individuals like the Thai fishermen, market vendors in Jakarta, factory workers in Seoul, office employees in Kuala Lumpur, and countless others across Asia created a ripple effect that was felt across the world. As once thriving economies plunged into deep recessions, the people, beleaguered yet resilient, adapted and responded. In the words of Robert Kiyosaki, "Financial crisis occurs when the rich don't play their money game correctly and the poor pay a hefty price."

In the bustling markets of Indonesia, traders switched to barter system when the Rupiah's value plummeted, underlining their innate survival instincts when the currency in their wallet turned inconsequential. Meanwhile, in Malaysia, citizens put their faith in the government's controversial decision to peg the Ringgit to the US Dollar, a decision that still sparks debates in economic corridors.

On the flipside, we see sparkle of hope and resilience in the cases like in South Korea where people queued up to donate their precious gold jewelry to help their nation recuperate its sinking reserves - a heartwarming act of patriotism that resonates even today. This reminds us of Mahatma Gandhi's quote, "A small body of determined spirits fired by an unconquerable faith in their mission can alter the course of history."

By analysing these diverse reactions, we are granted valuable insights into how policy decisions unfurl in the real economy and how real people adapt, cope, rebel or embrace. This exploration illuminates how the 'dismal science' transitions from cold theory to warm, living reality. As we move forward, let's keep these stirring anecdotes in mind, adding a humane touch to our understanding of Asia's financial foothold.

We invite you onboard this enlightening journey, not solely as an impartial observer, but an engaged participant. For the knowledge you gain from the past can indeed guide the decision you make for the future. As the famous saying goes, "History doesn't repeat itself, but it does often rhyme."

Sectoral Analysis

In the fervent whirlwind of Asia's ascending financial prominence, there lies a lesser-explored heartland - the arena of sectoral economies and how they dance with the tune of currency trends.

Sun Tzu, a Chinese military strategist, once said, "Know thy self, know thy enemy. A thousand battles, a thousand victories." Although cited in a different context, the essence of this quote remains highly relevant in the realm of economics. Recognizing the importance of foreknowledge, our sectoral analysis aims to arm you with a comprehensive understanding of how various sectors in Asian economies react and adapt to currency fluctuations.

Peel back the complex curtain of Asia's financial scene, and you will uncover intricate tales of cause-effect relationships woven into the everyday lives of ordinary people. Take for instance the powerful story of the Malaysian palm oil industry. The industry has a fierce reputation for resilience in the face of downsizing trends in global commodities. But, when the value of Ringgit took a sudden plunge in late 2016, export revenues skyrocketed, thus painting a silver lining around the ominous cloud. The oil palm farmers, nestled within the country's rural expanse, suddenly found themselves the unlikely benefactors of a large-scale economic tremor.

Such revealing anecdotes open our eyes to the elasticity of sectors when shaken by the ripple of currency change. Each sector bears a unique narrative of a struggle, survival, and sometimes an unexpected triumph, providing a fresh perspective to our cognizance of the macro-economic landscape.

Then we have instances of government intervention, as seen in the world's largest textile manufacturer, China, where currency manipulation was perceived as a weapon to sustain its lead. Currency devaluation reduced the cost of Chinese goods in the global market and sprung the textile industry to unprecedented heights. Through tactics that pitted economics against ethics, the "Middle Kingdom" proved what John Maynard Keynes meant when he observed, "The important thing for government is not to do things which individuals are doing already, and to do them a little better or a little worse, but to do those things which at present are not done at all."

Digging into these stories of upheaval and resilience, struggles and victories, this section embraces an endeavor to decipher these complex relationships between currencies and sectors. As we navigate the nuanced passageways of Asia's economic maze, we attempt to provide you more than just a financial analysis - we aim to acquaint you with the life pulse of Asia's economic powerhouse, the heart that allows it to not merely survive but thrive amidst the unpredictable tides of global finance.

Sectoral analysis unravels as a rich tapestry of intertwined narratives, a dance of numbers choreographed in the grand theatre of economics. It brings us face-to-face with the truth of not only how currency trends command the sectoral tunes but also how sometimes the sectors manage to lead. As we flip through the pages, remember this: the strength of economies always boils down to the creative strategies of survival, much like Ernest Hemingway said, "The world breaks everyone, and afterward, some are strong at the broken places." In the vast panorama of Asia's economy, are our sectors those stronger ones? Let us delve into these narratives and discover.

Future Projections

Future projections have the unique allure of a crystal ball. In the world of finance, they're our best guess at what's around the corner. Let's tread forth to unravel the impending economic shifts in Asia and scrutinize their global implications.

Few places have the economic momentum—or the potential to significantly sway global prosperity—than Asia. Marin Katusa, a global investor of some renown, once quipped, "The sheer scale of Asian dominance of future growth means that it's not particularly important what happens in the West; the East will succeed anyway." Perhaps Katusa knew the pendulum of economic power had started making its long arc towards Asia.

A popular anecdote in current financial circles tells us of a rather witty conversation between two seasoned economists, over a friendly game of golf. One remarked, "It's incredible how much the global economic axis has shifted, isn't it? It's like the center of gravity is moving eastward." The other, in the throes of his perfect swing, retorted, "Yes, my friend, and it doesn't seem like it's going to stop anytime soon."

This light-hearted exchange underscores a sobering reality: economic power, influenced by robust and prevalent industry, technical innovation, and emerging markets, is steadily tilting towards Asia.

With China leading the charge in establishing a fresh world economic order, one might argue that this sweeping change was ignited by Deng Xiaoping's 'Open Door' policy in 1978. Deng famously announced, "It doesn't matter whether a cat is black or white, as long as it catches mice." Translated: the ideological color (whether socialist or capitalist) is insignificant as long as it produces economic benefits.

Riding this wave of prosperity, other Asian nations like India,

Vietnam, and Indonesia too are poised to join the ranks of major global economies, triggering consequences far-reaching and deep.

As the financial sediments settle in on this shifting landscape, we observe an intriguing possibility. A combination of a growing middle class, rapid urbanization, and digital disruption could make Asia home to some of the world's largest consumer markets - thereby posing significant opportunities for local and global businesses alike.

Predicting the waves in such an ocean of possibility is notoriously tricky, but one cannot ignore the mounting evidence for Asia's ascendancy. However, it would be wise to keep in mind the words of John Kenneth Galbraith, "The only function of economic forecasting is to make astrology look respectable."

In the chapters that follow, we will take this prediction with a pinch of salt and explore the knots and nuances of Asia's financial footprint on the global landscape, a journey into the unpredictable mire that is the world economy. As we thread through theories and terms, anecdotes and insights, remember: in the world of finance, fortune favors the vigilant. Let's turn the page...

EUROPE'S FISCAL TAPESTRY

Euro Introduction

In the climactic tapestry of Europe's fiscal history, the pinnacle thread undoubtedly reads 'Euro Introduction'. A point in time that radically changed the economic landscape, not only of Europe, but also around the world, sending ripples across the global financial mirage.

Perhaps there is no better way to comprehend the detonating effect of this monumental event than to reminisce Roger Bootle's words, an eminent British economist and author, who famously said, "The whole idea that you can take sixteen, seventeen economies of vastly differing economic performance and put them all in one monetary policy straitjacket—that's a very dramatic, radical thing to have done."

So, let's embolden our economic curiosity and voyage back to the turbulent tides of the late 20th century—1999 to be precise. The stage was set. Years of diplomatic deliberations, strenuous negotiations, and tenacious groundwork culminated in the heralding of a new era—an era stamped with what we now recognise as the Euro.

Start this journey with the anecdotal recounting of the late former German Chancellor, Helmut Kohl, fondly dubbed as "The father of the Euro". This story, set in the backdrop of a united Berlin, stands as a testament of sheer ambition and consequential decision-making. Kohl, an astute political maestro, played a symphony of compelling dialogue and financial manoeuvring, paving the way for the inception of the common currency. He famously stated, "The introduction of the Euro can be compared to planting a seed. If the seed thrives and matures, it can provide shelter, if not, it becomes a wasted effort and a lost cause."

The story of the Euro's introduction illuminates the labyrinth of Europe's fiscal tapestry, revealing the bold decisions, shocking turnarounds and diplomatic chess plays that catapulted Europe onto a new financial horizon. As we delve deeper, we'll discover how this shared monetary project harmonised yet destabilized economies, vanquished yet fortified borders, sparked optimism yet incited challenges. And from this vantage point, we'll gain fresh perspectives, deciphering how we, the denizens of the global economic framework, can navigate this complex and ever-shifting terrain.

Fasten your seatbelts, readers, as we undertake a thrilling expedition that will reveal the riveting narrative behind the Euro's introduction. An exploration that elevates the possibilities and outcomes of economic decision-making to a realm that goes beyond just numbers and figures. For as credited economist J.K. Galbraith once mused, "The study of money, above all other fields in economics, is one in which complexity is used to disguise truth or to evade truth, not to reveal it." Let us embark to reveal those truths, one chapter at a time.

Brexit's Blow

Now we dive into the complex tapestry of Europe's fiscal landscape. The void in this pattern we now explore, is the result of a divisive decision shaking the continent to its core, Brexit. The chapter 'Europe's Fiscal Tapestry' takes a winding journey through the ups and downs of European fiscal decisions, and now, we turn to a section that can best be described as an earthquake in the European market - 'Brexit's Blow'.

A plethora of meanings could be drawn from the term "Brexit," but its essence lies in an act of separation, a pivotal point in the history of United Kingdom. The butterflies of change that flapped their wings in Britain have indeed set off a tempest across the continent. As Queen Elizabeth II famously said, "Grief is the price we pay for love." It seems that for a significant part of the European economy, Brexit has ushered in a period of grief as it came with a hefty cost.

When the news of the Brexit vote broke, a profound sense of uncertainty swept over the markets. The pound sterling, once the pride of the British economy, crumbled before our eyes. Its shaky descent was mirrored by raised eyebrows and furrowed contemplations in boardrooms across the world. In one dramatic overnight plunge, the sterling was wearing a label it had not worn since 1985 - the lowest value currency in the world.

Remembering those initial days, an anecdote comes to mind that encapsulates the frantic nature this decision induced. A hedge fund manager, shook by the upheaval, had likened the mood in the City of London to that of a football match. "Imagine," he said, "the final minutes of a tied championship game. Now imagine, the goalkeeper has left the field. The defense is lost, and everyone is running around like headless chickens. That was the city on the day after the vote."

There are myriad tales of uncertainty, tons of graphs indicating economic disparity, and lingering questions surrounding the United Kingdom's decision to part ways with the European Union. As we unravel 'Brexit's Blow', we provide not just figures, data and analyses of economic trends, but the stories behind them, the human responses and society's adaptive maneuvers. Our aim is not merely to shed light on the facts, but also to humanize them, to present a vivid picture of the world we live in, a world that is as much about numbers as it is about narratives. As we traverse through this section, let us recall the words of renowned British philosopher Alan Watts, "The only way to make sense out of change is to plunge into it, move with it, and join the dance."

In what follows, we will dance through the uncertainty, the upheavals, and the rebuilding in the aftermath of Brexit. The canvas of Europe's fiscal tapestry might appear somewhat worn and torn, but it is these imperfections and challenges that make the narrative incredibly compelling. So, let's turn the page and dive into the dance that is 'Brexit's Blow.'

Policy Playground

Beginnings often have gentle ways of stirring our sentiments. As we turn the pages of Europe's history, we encounter an elaborate mosaic of fiscal policy decisions, entrenched in the distinct socio-political landscape of each nation, making up the tapestry we see today. Now we delve into the nuances of policy decisions in Europe and their far-reaching implications on its economic health.

Picture it like a football match, where policymakers are the conductors orchestrating the game—and just as every pass, save, and strike matter—a single policy shift can tilt the economic scales abruptly. This narrative becomes even more intriguing no sooner than we let the echoes of Milton Friedman, the stalwart economist, reverberate in our ears: "One of the great mistakes is to judge policies and programs by their intentions rather than their results."

Recollect the financial crisis of 2008. The tumultuous times held a mirror up to Europe's financial vulnerability—an urgent nudge to revisit policy decisions made earlier. It was the time when austerity measures became the talk of the town. The constraints on public spending took a toll on the common man. "The hardest thing to learn in life is which bridge to cross and which to burn," said Bertrand Russell, yet this was exactly what Europe's economic policymakers were forced to reckon with. From Greece to Portugal, Germany to Ireland, individuals had to bear the brunt of those tough calls. Austerity was not just a policy for them, but a life-altering occurrence.

The narrative shifts to the adoption of the euro by a number of European countries—another impactful decision that sounded quite feasible theoretically. However, it inadvertently put the economically weaker countries in a straightjacket, limiting their ability to manipulate their currency in times of need. This can be a reminder of the wise words of Albert Einstein - "A theory remains a theory until proven in the field."

Europe's policy playground is a terrain where the games of power, economy, and social welfare are played, with each move echoing in the heartbeat of the continent. Walking along these lines, we explore the role played by European Central Bank's policies in the economic health of the countries under its influence - from setting interest rates that affect the investment behaviors to conducting operations that influence money supply.

As we continue on this exploratory journey, let's remember what Mark Twain once said: "History never repeats itself, but it often rhymes." While policy decisions are invariably context-tailored, the learnings derived can certainly wave the light for the path forward. The Policy Playground, hence, is not a relic of past decisions but rather an ever-evolving entity shaping Europe's future economic health.

So, tighten your seatbelts and fasten your mind's doors as we set about untangling the threads that weave Europe's Fiscal Tapestry. Together, we will trace the cause and effect, the action and reaction of this policy playground on the European economic health, echoing the Greek philosopher Heraclitus's timeless truth: "The only constant in life is change."

Navigating Crises

It was Winston Churchill who famously quipped, "Never let a good crisis go to waste." This sentiment rings especially true when we delve into the economic fabric of Europe, a fascinating tapestry that has been continually patched, torn, and mended again throughout the times of financial turbulence.

When we embark on this journey through the nooks and crannies of Europe's fiscal labyrinth, we soon realize that crisis navigation here isn't a mere reaction to catastrophic events. It becomes a defining element of the narrative itself. In the world of economics, crises are not just obstacles but also formidable teachers, providing lessons that can serve as lighthouses amidst the stormy seas of uncertainty.

The financial spectacle unraveled dramatically in Greece, like a Sophoclean drama, during the sovereign debt catastrophe of 2010, catapulting it into the hall of notoriety. Despite being a minnow in the European economic arena, Greece played the part of the butterfly that caused a hurricane, changing the perceptions about crisis navigation forever.

An anecdote to ponder in this saga would be the story of Antonis, a Greek carpenter who ran his family business in Athens. With the crisis worsening, the pillars of Antonis's world trembled under the weight of harsh austerity measures, and devastating cutbacks. But like many Greeks, Antonis demonstrated resilience. He migrated his business online, dealt in cash to mitigate the severe capital controls and began trading goods instead of purchasing, allowing his business to stay afloat. His story did not just showcase the gritty reality of crisis navigation at the grassroots level, but also displayed how innovation, adaptability, and resilience can shine through in the darkest of times.

In these trying periods, as businesses like Antonis's had

to reinvent themselves, the economic mandarins across the continent were also forced to rethink their strategies for crisis navigation. As Jean Monnet, one of the founding fathers of the European Union, posited: "Europe will be forged in crises and will be the sum of the solutions adopted for those crises." Central to these solutions is the European Central Bank (ECB), which took unprecedented steps to stimulate the economy, playing a pivotal role in ensuring stability and cushioning blows during hard times.

Exploring crisis navigation strategies introduces us to concepts crucial in understanding the workings of European economies. It underscores the importance of such concepts as austerity measures, debt restructuring, fiscal stimulus, bailouts, and the complex interplay between these factors.

As we journey through Europe's winding fiscal landscape, let's remember the wisdom of economist John Kenneth Galbraith: "The real accomplishment of modern science and technology consists in taking ordinary men, equipping them with good equipment, and enabling them to do extraordinary things." When we equip ourselves with the knowledge and understanding of crisis navigation, we too, can navigate these extraordinary events confidently and adeptly.

Every crisis, every hiccup in the economy is a new opportunity for growth, an invitation to rethink, re-strategize, and emerge stronger. In this section we browse through the lessons etched in the annals of Europe's economic history and aim to find meaning, understanding, and perspective amidst the tumultuous symphony of crises. Because as Churchill concluded, we should never let a good crisis go to waste.

Migration Matters

Migration matters. For centuries, humans have been crossing borders, traversing treacherous terrains, and navigating tumultuous waters in search of a better life. Regardless of distance or danger, the inexorable pull of promise is a force that is intuitively understood by anyone who has ever dreamed of a brighter future. No region on earth perhaps best encapsulates this saga of human migration and its multi-faceted impacts than Europe.

The European expanse bears witness to the defining moments charting the history of human mobility. From the eastward journeys of the analytic Greeks, medieval monks evangelizing across the continent, to today's economic immigrants and refugees, migration has shaped the geographical tapestry, sociocultural nuances and fiscal dynamics of Europe.

Basketball legend, Michael Jordan, once wisely said, "Talent wins games, but teamwork and intelligence win championships." Similarly, migration in Europe can be regarded not merely as the movement of bodies across geographical boundaries but the flow of talent, knowledge and culture, ultimately creating an environment rich in diversity and potential. Much like a championship game, it's not simply about moving the ball, but how those moves can create new paths, new strategies, and new victories.

Consider the story of Mina, an Iranian refugee woman who migrated to Sweden back in 1986 during the Iran-Iraq war. Today, Mina owns a thriving Persian restaurant in Stockholm providing employment opportunities to not just fellow Iranians, but Swedes as well. This not only showcases how migration can plant the seeds of entrepreneurship and employment but also emphasizes the cultural fusion brought about by these migrations. How many such Minas, we wonder, are integral threads to the flourishing fiscal tapestry of Europe? And how many more are waiting in the wings for an opportunity to contribute?

Historically and contemporarily, migration has been both a benefactor and a point of contention within Europe. One cannot talk about economic growth in cities like London, Berlin, or Barcelona without acknowledging the influence of migrant labor. Simultaneously, the debate around social integration and identity have grown in parallel, reflecting the cultural ebbs and flows of an ever-changing continent.

As renowned migration scholar, Stephen Castles, puts it, "Migration is a feature of social and economic life across many countries, but the profile of migrant populations varies considerably. In part this is because of the variety of sources of migration. In much of Europe, the migrant population is dominated by people who fled conflicts in their countries of origin." Indeed, conflict-induced migration and labor migration both contribute to the complex symphony of human movement that ultimately influences Europe's fiscal framework.

In thissection, we plan to navigate the intricate labyrinth of migration and its impacts on Europe's economies and societies. As we move forward, we will delve into the effects of migration, both benevolent and challenging, on employment, social integration, economic growth, and cultural exchange. We'll feature stories of individuals and communities that have had far-reaching effects on their adopted country's landscape, similar to the tale of Mina.

Migration, in essence, is a testament to human adaptability. It combines hope and hardship, dreams and dedication in a narrative, as old as mankind itself, and deeply imbued within Europe's fiscal tapestry. Both the triumphs and tribulations of migration illuminate a rich panorama of experiences that highlight crucial socioeconomic trends across the continent.

VIKRAM KUMAR

That's why migration matters.

Economic Ebb and Flow

Are you ready to embark on a fascinating journey through the undulating terrains of Europe's economy, where vast valleys of prosperity run alongside towering peaks of financial crises? Welcome to the section we lovingly named as 'Economic Ebb and Flow'. This is more than just a story about numbers and pie charts; it's a colourful tapestry of glistening prosperity, muted hardships, and the remarkable resilience of societies, all woven into the complex world of monetary policies and economic trends.

Let's commence our journey with a delightful Dutch saying - "Geld groeit niet aan de bomen". Has your mind started churning to decipher this? Well, it translates to the familiar proverb "Money doesn't grow on trees", underlining the inherent worth of economy and industry in a land known for tulips and Gouda cheese. More than just expressing the value of hard work, this proverb underscores a deeper understanding of economizing resources and the unstinting effort that goes into creating wealth - an understanding grounded in the thousand-year-old Dutch dealings with trade and finance.

History is full of incredible stories where great nations would navigate through quaking recessions, only to emerge stronger with a renewed vigour. Recall the era of the Spanish financial crisis that began in 2008, a time when 'La Crisis', as it was known, was more than a regular visitor, and seemed to have taken permanent residence in Spain. This was a period defined by heightened unemployment rates, increased national debt, and economic despair. Yet, it led to an era of remarkable innovation, resourcefulness, and resurgence. The story of Juan Moreno, a small scale entrepreneur during this time, is illustrative. Post losing his job in a large conglomerate, he ventured into setting up a small, environmentally-friendly hacksaw production factory which turned a good profit. Today, he employs 50 locals, and his story remains an unsung anthem of the financial crisis.

As we delve into these stories and anecdotes, we are reminded of the words of former American President, Bill Clinton, "When times are tough, constant conflict may be good politics but in the real world, cooperation works better." Europe, through its changing economic landscapes, has often embodied this spirit of cooperation. Whether through coordinated EU-wide fiscal stimuli during downturns, or through harmonious exchange of ideas and best practices, the European economies have proven that collective resilience can pave the way for individual prosperity.

Through the waves of Europe's economic past, present, and its vision for the future, we uncover tales of extraordinary resilience, unshakable determination, and unfaltering bouts of innovation. In 'Economic Ebb and Flow', you will navigate through stories of the sweeping power of financial policies, bear witness to the struggles of economic depression, and celebrate the triumphs of resilience. As you travel with us through Europe's enchanting economic journey, it's intriguing to see that the economic terrain has always been much more than a mere series of monetary transactions; it's a sizable chunk of human living, a testament to the unfaltering human spirit, and a seemingly endless saga of triumph over adversity.

Regional Ramifications

In the early 21st century, famed British geographer, Roger Brunet, remarked, "Nowhere else in the world do so many countries rub shoulders with each other without getting too familiar." I couldn't have found a more fitting way to begin our exploration of Europe's diverse fiscal tapestry. Now we shall traverse a panoply of European landscapes, not in a quest to appreciate their geographical charm, but to understand the differing consequences—some stinging, some beneficial—that economic trends have on these territories.

Our exploration begins in Southern Europe—Greece to be precise. Often dubbed the 'Cradle of Western Civilization,' Greece fell from its glorious heights to a less enviable pedestal— a beacon for national bankruptcy. The reason? An economic downfall triggered back in 2008, when Greece revealed that it had been understating its deficit figures, setting in motion a chain of events that saw it plunged into a severe financial crisis. This event, known as the Greek Financial Crisis, revealed the fragility among the Eurozone countries, emphasizing Brunet's apt depiction of the regional closeness yet fiscal distance.

In stark contrast, let's turn our gaze to the central region, to the titan that is Germany. Its power lies not in its size or military might, but in its economic strength. With a well-established manufacturing sector and a robust export economy, it managed to shield itself from the economic shocks that rattled its southern neighbors. As English economist John Maynard Keynes advised, "The important thing for Government is not to do things which individuals are doing already, and to do them a little better or a little worse; but to do those things which at present are not done at all." The German government's keen focus on bolstering industrial growth and fostering technological innovation is a testament to this philosophy, leading to a more resilient economy.

And what about Eastern Europe? Let's look at Poland. While not economically as strong as Germany, Poland emerged from the post-Soviet Era like a phoenix rising from the ashes. Its rapid transformation from a planned economy to a market-based one serves as an inspirational tale of recovery and resilience, especially when juxtaposed against the backdrop of regional neighbors grappling with economic instability.

Here we will dig deeper into these and more anecdotes from diverse regions, drawing insights on how macroeconomic landscapes influence the regional responses and adaptation strategies. We will explore how areas that were once economic backwaters have become engines for growth, while others, traditionally prosperous, have struggled to maintain their stature. We will use this journey to understand the complex, ever-evolving tapestry of Europe's economy, unraveling the secrets behind its resilience and resourcefulness.

As we embark on this journey investigating the 'Regional Ramifications,' let's bear in mind Brunet's words which underline the unique coexistence in Europe. This cultural and fiscal kaleidoscope serves as a fascinating study, helping us comprehend the intricacies of the much-discussed and deeply complicated theme of economic trends and their impact across this diverse continent known as Europe. So, buckle up and join me as we navigate the narrative of Europe's Fiscal Tapestry!

Voices from Various Venues

In the 'Voices from Various Venues' section of the book, we dive deep into the fray of public opinion, bringing you stories from across the European continent. Here, we explore the tapestry of opinions on economic policies and trends that forge and shape the realities of Europe's fiscal landscape. The opinions shared in this section are woven from diverse threads of society, from market analysts sequestered in high-rise offices to passionate activists raising their placards in protest.

Let us begin with a noteworthy anecdote from Spain. Meet Antonio, a spirited young man who works in the bustling markets of Valencia. One sunny afternoon at a local café, we asked Antonio about his thoughts on the European Central Bank's fiscal policies. He responded, "Inflation is eating us alive! We might as well be throwing away our money. It's like trying to fill up a bucket, but the bucket has a hole in it."

Through Antonio's perspective, we can glimpse the discontent brewing amongst citizens due to rising prices. As former US President Ronald Reagan once said, "Inflation is as violent as a mugger, as frightening as an armed robber, and as deadly as a hitman." Distilled in Antonio's words and echoed in Reagan's sentiment is the collective frustration of everyday citizens struggling to keep up with the juggernaut of the economy.

Moving northwards, we traverse to Germany, where we have an encounter with a completely different viewpoint. Hanna, a seasoned market analyst in Frankfurt, embodies the optimism often found in the corporate sector. Discussing the same fiscal policies, Hanna says, "Inflation? Yes, it's a challenge. But we are equipped, and the future looks promising. One must keep in mind that a bit of inflation stimulates spending, which drives our economy."

Hanna's statement is a testimonial to the steadfast faith in the economy's resilience, akin to former Chancellor Angela Merkel's belief that "The economy must serve people, not the other way around."

These two contrasting opinions demonstrate the deep societal divide when discussing Europe's fiscal policies. Through the narrative in 'Voices from Various Venues', the readers are privy to the chorus of diverse voices that shape Europe's economic narrative, a veritable symphony that ebbs and flows with every policy change and shift in market trends.

We will continue to enrich the narrative with personal anecdotes, experiences, and insights from every nook and corner, every market square or office building of our diverse tapestry of venues. We do this not merely for the sake of sharing stories but to breathe life into the heart of economic discourse, allowing for better comprehension, empathy, and potential change.

This section thus acts as a microcosm of the opinions reverberating throughout Europe, thereby enabling us to better navigate the global economic mirage. So, reader, we invite you to join us on this journey through the very heart of Europe's fiscal narrative, where we underpin the raw human emotions beneath the stiff figures and cold statistics that often dictate economic discourse.

AFRICAN ADVENTURES

Colonial Legacies

In the heart of the great African continent, tinged with the hues of its rich culture, vibrant traditions, and resplendent resources, exists an imprint of its colonial past. This past, as invigorating yet complex like the courses of the Nile, continues to shape the socioeconomic trajectory of Africa. As we embark on a fascinating journey through the vibrant streets of Africa's burgeoning metropolitan cities, we uncover the potent influences of colonial histories on today's African economies. The chapter ahead is akin to peeling back the layers of an onion - the deeper we delve into Africa's financial fabric, the more tears of poignant revelations it conjures.

Colonialism, an interplay of power, control, and resource extraction has had a profound impact on Africa. The lucid words of Walter Rodney, author and passionate advocate of Pan-Africanism, reverberate through the epochs, reminding us, "In colonial Africa, direct political control by European governments combined with raw economic exploitation." From Angola's oil deposits to the diamond mines of Sierra Leone, which European powers hawkishly eyed, the legacies of colonialism thread heavy, yet meaningful patches onto Africa's economic tapestry.

One cannot ignore an enduring anecdote of the Belgian rule in Congo. Its flag wasn't the blue, yellow, and red we recognize today; it was a relentless grey of unrelenting abuse and plunder. This tale of the 'Rubber Terror' resounds through Congo till today. Congo, a landlocked country crammed full of rubber trees, was whipped into submission, their uniquely useful resource exploited to serve the Belgian economy. Yet today, while Belgium's streets might gleam with the prosperity reaped from this exploitation, Congo's economy trudges, bearing the burdens of its sullen history.

Yet, colonial fingerprints don't merely embody a history of exploitation. In many parts of Africa, colonists imposed a Western-style economy - an attempt to dress the African spirit in a new persona. Whether these new clothes fit or not, that's a debate still splitting hairs amongst economists. Kenya, once the bedrock of the British Empire, reaped both the wrath and wealth of colonial economic policies. Today, Kenya stands tall amongst Africa's biggest economies, with a thriving service sector and well structured, albeit an often-criticized, currency system.

The great Nelson Mandela once said, "It always seems impossible until it's done." As the African economies grapple with the aftermath of colonial legacies, they face a complex tapestry of immense potential interspersed with formidable challenges. As we travel deeper into the African heart through the following chapters, remember Mandela's words, for, in Africa, the possibilities are as boundless as the horizon beneath the African sun.

Commodity Challenges

For many, the mere mention of Africa conjures up images of magnificent wildlife, vast plains, winding rivers, and dense jungles. But as Edward Abbey, the renowned American writer and environmental advocate, once said, "Wilderness is not a luxury, but a necessity of the human spirit." And just like the wilderness, Africa isn't just a place of geographic marvels; it's an untamed economic powerhouse, a dynamic and pulsating heart that propels the global economy in a myriad of crucial commodities.

Now we'll delve deep into Africa's beating economic heart, unraveling the intricacies of the role commodities play in shaping the continent's economic trends.

Picture yourself settling into a warm, inviting armchair by the fireplace, a delicate and sizeable cappuccino steaming beside you. The slight bitterness of the coffee runs down your throat, a bitter testament to the struggles of the African coffee farmers. Situated in the fertile highlands of Ethiopia, these farmers are at the mercy of the global coffee market, their livelihoods oscillating with the ebb and flow of international demand and fluctuating prices.

However, this is not just a story of vulnerability, but also of resilience. As the Ugandan economist and philosopher Andrew Mwenda would often quote, "Africa's story is not just about challenges; it is about spirited individuals and societies who, in the face of monumental odds, choose to press forward." Amidst the turmoil of the coffee market, one envisages the story of Abed Bwanika, a coffee farmer who, despite the uncertainty of the coffee trade, adapted and thrived. Innovation became the name of the game, with farmers like Bwanika investing in new machines for better yield and collaborating with international partners to access broader markets.

Their fascinating tale of survival and triumph is representative of a wider trend. For within Africa's economic landscape, commodities have posed not just challenges but opportunities, catalyzing transformational shifts in policies and practices, impacting the lives of millions.

There is a Swahili saying that goes "Kidole kimoja hakivunji chawa", "One finger cannot kill a louse". Here, the louse is the overarching challenge that Africa faces in the global commodity market, and the fingers symbolize the collective efforts needed to overcome it. No single entity can effectively challenge or change the complex global commodity system on their own; it'll require collective regional efforts, international partnerships, and innovative solutions.

Let us delve into the heart of commodity challenges in Africa, uncovering not just the struggles, but the triumphs, the moments of despair and hope, the setbacks and comebacks. For Africa is not merely a passive player in the global commodity chessboard; she is a dynamic force, reinventing the rules of the game with each passing day.

Navigating Volatility

In the seemingly incoherent mosaic of African economic landscape, one pattern invariably stands out - the potent drumbeat of volatility. Fueled by factors as diverse as fluctuating oil prices, erratic rainfall and periodic political instability, this volatility defines and shapes businesses, policymaking, and indeed, the very lives of the people on the continent.

Take for example, Nigeria, a nation blessed, and simultaneously cursed, with an abundance of oil. When global oil prices nosedive, so does the country's economy, plunging its citizens into hardships. But amidst these difficulties emerge some of the most resilient and creative entrepreneurs the world has ever seen. The story of Ngozi, a young Nigerian woman, is a shining testament to this. When oil prices crashed in 2016, leaving her family teetering on the edge of poverty, Ngozi took matters into her own hands. With little capital and no business experience, she set up a neighborhood grocery store. Today, it's a thriving enterprise providing employment to local youth and a vast selection of affordable goods for the local community.

Nelson Mandela once said, "I learned that courage was not the absence of fear, but the triumph over it. The brave man is not he who does not feel afraid, but he who conquers that fear ". Ngozi's journey embodied this spirit, as she deftly navigated economic volatility, turning adversities into opportunities.

However, volatility, when managed effectively, can become a key lever for growth. One cannot discuss the economic trajectory of Africa, without mentioning Ethiopia. With its robust public infrastructure development and proactive government policies, Ethiopia has shown the world that there's a way to tame the beast of volatility and create positive economic growth.

Notably, during 2009 to 2019, Ethiopia safeguarded its people from the worst effects of an erratic climate by deploying an innovative strategy - a large-scale, national, social-protection program called the Productive Safety Net Programme (PSNP). This program provides cash or food to millions of people in exchange for their work on public infrastructure projects. When drought hit Ethiopia in 2011, instead of spiraling into a catastrophic famine as in the past, PSNP acted as a buffer, enhancing the resilience of its economy and people.

As Zelda la Grange, Nelson Mandela's personal aide, put it, "Africa was not for sissies". Perhaps nowhere else in the world is economic resilience so strikingly manifest as in Africa. Volatility may be a perpetual companion, but the indomitable spirit and inventive strategies of Africans, effectively repurpose it as a catalyst for extraordinary outcomes and opportunities. The journey then becomes not about eliminating volatility, but learning to dance in its rhythmic fluctuations, defying fear and daring immense possibilities.

In the forthcoming pages, we will continue to dive deeper into pragmatic strategies and real-life examples from across the African expanse that have effectively managed volatility, offering you a comprehensive framework to understand this striking play between adversity and opportunity. Buckle up, it's going to be a fascinating journey – revealing, stimulating and certainly, never mundane.

Hopeful Horizons

In the glorious sunrise of a new day, we find ourselves venturing into the fascinating realm of 'Hopeful Horizons', a section pulsating with promise under the sprawling canopy of 'African Adventures' in our financial odyssey. Expanding our horizons towards the potential future scenarios and opportunities nestled within the rustic beauty of African economies, this segment promises a journey of discovery, deviations, and deliberate decisions.

As we set forth on this expedition, we let the wise words of economist, Paul Romer, guide us: "A crisis is a terrible thing to waste." Indeed, Africa, for long marred by financial crises, today presents itself as a continent bubbling with possibilities, young energetic labor, bountiful natural resources, and evolving technological frontiers. The journey forward may be arduous, but a hopeful horizon is emerging.

To illuminate the profound opportunities, let us delve into an anecdotal snippet from Rwanda, a shining beacon of African progress. In the aftermath of the horrifying 1994 genocide, Rwanda found itself at two crossroads: one that led to prolonged despair, and the other towards a painstaking but rewarding resurrection. Choosing the latter, it embraced socio-economic reforms with resilience and determination so fierce that today, a mere three decades later, Rwanda is a robust economy, one that's banking on smart technology and innovation for sustainable growth.

This story exemplifies the indomitable African spirit - echoed in the inspiring words of the late Kofi Annan, "We may have different religions, different languages, different colored skin, but we all belong to one human race." It's precisely this shared humanity and spirit that could drive African economies towards a hopeful horizon.

Ghana, another intriguing story in Africa's financial tapestry, could be seen through the eyes of a small local cocoa farmer. Struggling under the weight of fluctuating global cocoa prices, his breakthrough came in the shape of innovative government backed financing schemes. Through these, the farmer didn't just survive but thrived, transforming his small cocoa plantation into a flourishing enterprise. His individual success story mirrors the potential of sensible economic policies impacting grassroots levels of society, further influencing the national economy.

The story of African economies is like a diamond in the rough. They present a unique blend of traditional wisdom and modern aspirations. This financial landscape teeters on an exciting threshold where immense potential waits to be unearthed from its rich mines of human resources and natural wealth. As we navigate through this mirage of global finance, we may find that Africa, once deemed the 'dark continent', potentially holds the key to a luminous future.

As Nelson Mandela once said, "It always seems impossible until it's done. In this beautiful harmony unfolds the latent promise of Africa's forthcoming financial zenith. The journey won't be simple, but the hopeful horizons beckon. It's time we heed the call.

Personal Perspectives

As the morning sun peered over the horizon, bomas scattered across the vast African plains began to show signs of life. This mesmerizing panorama brims with untold stories – stories of life, survival, resilience, and indomitably human spirits, stories that are distinctly woven into the rich tapestry of Africa's economic journey. This is where our African adventures begin – with 'Personal Perspectives'. Here, we seek to delve into the real, intimate narratives of those living in the heart of Africa to understand the profound impact of economic policies on their daily lives.

"The welfare of the people in particular has always been the alibi of tyrants," Albert Camus once remarked. His words echo in the heart of Africa, a continent that has grappled with the repercussions of economic manipulations disguised as growth policies. While this section is steeped in honesty and the raw grit of reality, it's also an ode to resilience, capturing the extraordinary strength of ordinary men and women navigating the unchartered waters of economic disparities.

One such anecdote brings us to Asha, a mother of three in Tanzania. In the bustling local markets of Dar es Salaam, Asha haggles her way through the day, buying vegetables and spices to grind into a one-of-a-kind spice mix. Increased taxation and inflation rates have hit her small enterprise hard, forcing her to grind extra hours into the night just to make ends meet. Yet, Asha's spirit remains uncrushable, her hope as infectious as her laughter. "These spices teach me about life, about patience and persistence," she says. Asha's story is a testament to perseverance, one amid many that we unearth in our journey.

Through the lens of stories like Asha's, we seek to uncover how individuals negotiate the labyrinth of economic policies, their triumphs and their turmoils. Such personal perspectives, oftentimes overlooked, paint a vivid picture of the multifaceted impacts of global financial conspiracies.

Amidst tales of struggle, we also find inspiring narratives of innovation. Take, for example, the young tech entrepreneurs of Nairobi turning the city into Africa's 'Silicon Savannah'. These individuals harness the power of digital technology to leapfrog traditional economic barriers, defying odds and altering narratives.

As the noted economist John Maynard Keynes professed, "There is no subtler, no surer means of overturning the existing basis of society than to debauch the currency." Thus, throughout this chapter, we'll explore how people like Asha and the techies of Nairobi dance within this tumultuous economic space, reshaping society one innovation, one spice blend, one day at a time.

The stories nestling within this book, like a perfect blend of Asha's spices, are a rich assortment of tales that encapsulate resilience, innovation, and the human spirit fighting against financial odds. Personal Perspectives provokes not just thought, but also emotions, giving you a first-row view on the grand stage of economic living.

In this journey, my dear reader, brace yourself for a crash course in economics unlike any other - no jargons, no graphs, no confusion. Just stories. Human stories. For in the grand scheme of the financial world, it is the individual tales that truly define the currency conspiracy.

So, let's delve into these narratives and navigate the global financial mirage, one personal perspective at a time.

Community Chronicles

"Money may make the world go round, but community is the axle upon which it spins," an old African proverb echoes. It's the collective verve of communities that moulds the formless sand dunes of economic trends into distinctive landscapes. As we delve into the 'Community Chronicles', we shall navigate through the nitty-gritties of African communities, and unravel how economic trends—and 'economic mirages'—build or break them.

In the sun-drenched terrain of Africa, where solidarity is the lifeline and kinship the heartbeat, economic nuances bind together the diverse facets of communities like intricate beadwork. Let me share an anecdote, not just any anecdote, but one that was sung to me with heartfelt fervour by Marjani, a tireless mother and entrepreneur from the bustling markets of Dakar, Senegal.

Marjani, radiating warmth and indomitable spirit, was a woman whose life had been embroidered with the colourful threads of adversity and triumph, woven together to create the rich tapestry of her existence. When the global economy nose-dived in the late 2000s, Marjani's small grocery business was caught in the tumultuous tide. However, amid this chaotic dance of economic variables, Marjani, like many others in her community, arose. She understood that "in crisis, there is opportunity," harnessing the economic unrest as a catalyst for communal growth.

She invited her neighbours, who were also battling similar trials, to pool resources and create a co-operative—a little ark to save them from the stormy economic seas. This co-op didn't merely survive the storm; it throve, transforming their struggle for survival into a voyage of communal prosperity.

Depicted against the backdrop of the global economic facade,

Marjani's story serves as a microcosm of the resilience and ingenuity of communities grappling with economic trends. The collective ethos of African communities births bright sparks of innovation and resilience which defy the shadows of economic uncertainty.

As we embark on this riveting journey through the 'Community Chronicles', we will find ourselves seated around the communal fire, trading tales of economic mirages under the vast African sky. Some may be melancholic serenades of struggle, while others, jubilant symphonies of triumph. What they all share, though, according to the wise words of Nigerian Nobel Laureate Wole Soyinka, is the unyielding spirit of humanity: "A tiger does not shout its tigritude, it acts."

In the pages to follow, you'll come to appreciate that even in the throes of economic torrents and tremors, communities are more than mere spectators. They're active participants in the ancient dance of survival and prosperity, weaving the winds of economic trends into their societal fabric.

So, dear readers, tighten your grip, sharpen your senses, and brace yourself for an entrancing foray into the Community Chronicles as we traverse the African landscape, painting portraits of communities dancing with the fickle mirage of economic trends. After all, "The world is a book, and those who do not travel read only one page." Let's turn the page, shall we?

Economic Entanglements

Let's embark on an uncharted terrain, dive deep into an arena most dare not to wander into, the complex world of African economies and their connection to global trends. Gird your loins as we uncover the intricate threading of policies, fluctuating markets, and the seemingly invisible underwater tectonics that construct the African economic landscape.

In the late morning of a hot June day, under the relentless African sun, a busy marketplace in Lagos, Nigeria, offers a sight to behold. The cacophony of bargaining voices, the vibrancy of colorful fabrics fluttering in the wind, and the aroma of pepper soup simmering on hot coals - a scenario that seems mundane but is deeply intertwined with the global economic narrative.

Speaking of narratives, have you ever wondered how the price of a bowl of soup in Lagos might be tied to a stock exchange in Wall Street or the GDP of China? This is the story of interconnectedness that has come to define the global economic ecosystem in the 21st century.

As Thomas L. Friedman put it, "The hidden hand of the market will never work without a hidden fist." And Africa's economic empowerment and self-reliance require the dexterity of dodging that fist while allowing the hand to direct, subtly influencing the course of the market.

African policy-makers, after all, are locked in a lyrical dance with counterparts worldwide, a subtle Waltz that influences trade regulations, currencies mechanisms, even local inflation rates. It's these precise steps, these low bows and twirls that shape the fate of economies, outlining booms and signaling recessions.

Consider the story of Kenya's 'M-Pesa', a mobile payment system that transformed East African economies. This ingenious innovation has become a global model, influencing financial technological trajectories far and wide, including far-off places like India and Afghanistan. Yet, it is these very global influences that could cause M-Pesa's indigenous innovation to lose its foothold in its homeland to a dominantly Western financial architecture.

To quote Kofi Annan, "Knowledge is power. Information is liberating. Education is the premise of progress, in every society, in every family." As we dive into the heart of African economic landscapes, bringing to light the intricate tapestry of economic principles, groundbreaking innovations, and often-overlooked insights, we gain knowledge, understanding, and context. Knowledge brings power, and power brings the capacity to steer our world, no matter how subtly, towards a more equitable, prosperous, and sustainable future for all.

This journey traverses from the ears of maize growing in Malawi, through the cobalt mines in the Congo, and along the glowing corridors of Ethiopia's burgeoning tech startups. Crucially, our expedition illustrates how a continent traditionally viewed as economically marginal is painstakingly crafting the stitching that binds the global economy's cloak.

Hold onto your hats, dear readers. We are about to delve headfirst into the quicksilver realm of 'Economic Entanglements.'

Political Playbooks

In the heart of Africa, the history of political turmoil and economic turbulence are as intertwined as the mighty Nile River. 'Political Playbooks,' a section of the riveting 'African Adventures,' introduces readers to a world where political strategies significantly influence economic trends. To paraphrase the infamous Chinese philosopher, Confucius, "Everything under heaven is in utter chaos; the situation is excellent."

So, what do politics and economics have to do with each other? Well, everything!

"And whilst politics might be the driving force, it's economics that fuels the engine," once observed by a shrewd African market trader. His insight forms the cornerstone of our adventure through the tumultuous landscapes of African politics and economics, where survival and financial growth heavily depend on understanding the political playbook.

One of the most striking tales in this space comes from Zimbabwe, where a political decision in 2000 dramatically impacted the country's economy. When the government initiated a controversial land reform program, it intended to realign the racial imbalance in land ownership. Unfortunately, the move set off a chain reaction of events that led to hyperinflation, wiping out savings and pensions overnight.

What lesson does it teach us, you ask? Simply put, economic destruction or success lies in the hands of policy-making. Tanzania's late president, Julius Nyerere, put this into perspective when he wisely said, "Without peace, there is no development; without development, there is no peace."

For African nations, the political playbook isn't just about winning elections. It involves transforming policies into economic powerhouses. However, the wrong move might topple the house of cards, leading to economic ruin.

To navigate the treacherous waters of African political and economic strategies, one must understand the intricate game of chess that's in play. In such a world, every move counts; missteps can set the country back decades, whilst strategic decisions can thrust a nation towards a promising economic dawn.

Our journey across Africa is a testament to the renowned African proverb, "When the music changes, so does the dance." So come, navigate the intriguing global financial mirage through the diverse landscapes of African politics and dynamics. Understand how policies, strategies, politics, and economies dance to the rhythm of change and circumstance in this intriguing chapter called 'Political Playbooks.'

In the grand Chessboard of global politics and economics, the African adventures provide a gripping saga. It's an enduring dance of survival and prosperity, where political strategies choreograph economic outcomes. As we delve deeper, may we become wiser in understanding the eternal dance between politics and economics, realizing that each decision has a ripple effect, evident in the ebb and flow of global finance.

LATIN AMERICAN LIQUIDITY

Historical Handicaps

As we navigate the intriguing tunnel of Latin American economics in this segment, 'Historical Handicaps,' let us draw our attention to the bricks that build its wall - the myriad historical events that have painted this vibrant region with a palette of uncertainty, resilience, and a conviction to thrive.

Latin America, an exquisite mosaic of cultures, is a region known for its bountiful resource endowment. But as any economist would caution, 'resources are both a blessing and a curse.' The 'Curse of Plenty', an economic paradox, has been as palpable in Latin America as the warmth of its equatorial sun.

Let's revisit the 1970s, when the influx of 'petrodollars' sparked a period of easy loans and jubilant spending for Latin America. Oil-rich countries, awash with newfound wealth, needed banks to stash their cash, and American banks played their part. Eager to lend these petrodollars, Latin America, with its youthful optimism and resource-filled lands, was an appealing suitor. The result? A lending bonanza, one that Latin American countries reveled in. Until, as is often the case with economics, the tide turned...

Fast forward to the 1980s, a decade dubbed as Latin America's 'Lost Decade'. The Standard Oil founder, John D. Rockefeller, once quipped, "Do you know the only thing that gives me pleasure? It's to see my dividends coming in." Unfortunately, a time can be recounted in Latin America where dividends did anything but 'come in'. The lenders became restless, the dollar strengthened, interest rates spiked, and the house of cards that was Latin American debt, crumbled. The ripple effect of this economic catastrophe was poverty, unemployment, and angst.

However, history demands a nuance in its understanding. It isn't always about economic gloom. The tale of hyperinflation in Brazil brings forth an intriguing twist, a silver lining in a stormy cloud. Consider the 'Real Plan' in 1994 – an economic miracle that pulled Brazil out of an inflationary spiral by a unique experiment of launching a virtual currency. This bold move stabilized the economy, tamed inflation, and showed that sometimes innovative solutions come from dire challenges.

As we wind this chapter, a quote by Heraclitus, the Greek philosopher, encapsulates the essence of Latin America's economy, "Character is destiny." The region's economic character, shaped by its historical handicaps, has crafted a destiny of resilient adaptability. It teaches us to view Latin America beyond its stereotypical avatar, to the realm where history, culture, and economics intertwine, etching a vibrant economic tapestry.

Through Latin America's oscillating economic journey, each nation within has stood, stumbled, but ultimately has striven ahead. Every account is a reminder of our constant negotiation with history, of its tenacious grip on the present and the future.

Policy Pivots

In the pulsating heart of the global economic ecosystem, frequent policy pivots play an unmissable role, especially in the lively realm of Latin American liquidity. Each change in policy is like a stone thrown into a tranquil pond, creating ripples that spread across the surface, leaving profound and lasting turmoil in their wake. Our premise here is to examine how these ripples — both big and small — influence the economic health of Latin American nations.

Stories of such policy changes aren't confined to the dry pages of dour economics textbooks; they are the lifeblood of entire economies, affecting the lives of millions, influencing fortunes and futures, creating tragic tales and stories of staggering reversals.

Let's embark on this exploration with the anecdote of Argentina, which in the mid-20th century, stood shoulder to shoulder with the world's most prosperous nations. However, a series of policy missteps sent it spiraling down the world economic order. A daunting cautionary tale, yes, but one loaded with essential teachings and insights.

One cannot help but echo the words of British economist John Maynard Keynes when he famously stated, "The difficulty lies not so much in developing new ideas as in escaping from old ones." Argentina's financial downfall is a potent reminder of Keynes' wisdom - a stark demonstration of how clinging to outdated economic policies can wreak havoc on a country's financial health.

But, not all policy stories are somber. Take the case of Chile, for instance. Once crippled by hyperinflation and economic instability, Chile ones wrought a financial phoenix from the ashes of its dying economy. Their policy pivot, which involved shifting gears from state-controlled measures to market-oriented reforms, catapulted Chile into being one of the fastest-growing economies in Latin America.

Argentine author, Jorge Luis Borges, once wrote, "Reality is not always probable, or likely." The journey of Chile certainly underlines Borges' wisdom, taking the skeptical world by surprise, portraying the power of intentional and well-strategized policy changes.

The narrative of policy pivots is a riveting saga, filled with storms and sunshine, chaos, and calm. As we delve deeper into this section titled 'Policy Pivots,' we will navigate the labyrinth of these economic policy changes across various Latin American countries. We will explore how these deliberate economic maneuvers signal the ebb and flow of financial health, determining the economic prosperity or peril of these vibrant nations.

Join me in this expedition, as we unfold the intricate tapestry of Latin American liquidity, one policy change at a time.

Inflation and Instability

"Economists set themselves too easy, too useless a task if, in tempestuous seasons they can only tell us that when the storm is past, the ocean is flat again" - It was none other than the influential economist, John Maynard Keynes who uttered these words.

We take our first step on this voyage of discovery in the blistering heat of Latin America, a continent that has faced the full-brunt of economic turbulence time and again. A continent that, despite its challenges, has consistently risen from the ashes, much like the legendary phoenix. It's a prime model of the indomitable spirit of human endeavor in the face of adversity.

Let us take a moment to consider a typical shopping day in the bustling markets of Buenos Aires, Argentina. Maria, a 70-year-old retired teacher, meanders through crowded aisles, sweat trickling down her face, her gaze locked in an anxious dance between shelves laden with goods and the rapidly changing prices on the store's digital display. This was not a scene from a dystopian novel but a stark reality experienced by Argentinians during the gripe inflationista, the inflation grip, a period of economic instability that had private families bearing the brunt of skyrocketing prices.

The tale of Maria and her fellow Argentinians is not mere anecdotal evidence of an isolated incident. It's representative of a pervasive issue that has spread its roots deep within the very fabric of Latin American society. Think of the hyperinflation crisis in Venezuela. Once a symbol of prosperity and abundant natural resources, the oil-rich nation was plunged into chaos, its citizens brought to their knees by crippling economic instability.

The famed economist Milton Friedman once said, "Inflation is taxation without legislation." Friedman's words ring particularly true in the context of Latin America: countless citizens found their purchasing power relentlessly eroded by the silent thief that is inflation. The instability caused was not only on an economic level, but also sociopolitical.

Our journey in this section, while braving the tumultuous waters of Latin American economics, is not merely aimed at delineating the problem. It's far more ambitious, aiming to dissect the complex interplay of factors that give rise to such situations, to mitigate, if not prevent, the future recurrence of similar economic catastrophes. It's about unearthing the lessons that could be gleaned from the past, and arming ourselves with knowledge and insight as we navigate the uncertain terrains of the global financial mirage.

In the words of Benjamin Franklin, "An investment in knowledge pays the best interest." As we delve into the tangled web of Latin American Inflation and Instability, we hope to make that investment for our readers – an investment that will prove worthwhile on their journey through the global financial landscape.

Commerce

Latin America – a vibrant canvas of culture, color, and, crucially, commerce. The rhythms of trade beat loudly across this vast and diverse expanse, telling chronicles of prosperity, adversity, resilience, and transformation. In this realm, the footprints of global policy bounds resonate into an intricate tango – a dance intertwined with the tale of Latin American economics.

Once upon a time, prolific Argentinian writer Jorge Luis Borges said, "Reality is not always probable, or likely." Strangely, these words ring true when it comes to understanding the implications carved by the knife of global trade on Latin America's economic contour. Borges might not have been a economist, but his perceptive sentiment paints a vivid picture of the complex landscape of Latin America's trade scenario.

Consider Chile's copper industry, for example. The nation's tales of copper could easily rival the Bolivian folklore in terms of passion and intrigue. Once upon a policy shift, the global copper markets dipped erratically. Chile, as the world's largest copper producer, was forced to tap dance on a tightrope. When copper prices rebounded, though, the nation did more than merely survive - it saw an unprecedented economic surge. Like the mythical phoenix rising from the ashes, Chile's fiscal scenario rejuvenated – a stark testament to Latin American resiliency.

Then there's the tale of Mexico, a country straddling the line between tradition and trade – cultures steeped in age-old tradition on one side and economic progression driven by foreign influence on the other. After signing the North American Free Trade Agreement (NAFTA), the Mexican economy transformed, becoming an industrial powerhouse. Mexican author Carlos Fuentes aptly said, "Recognize yourself in he and she who are not like you and me." This quote quietly echoes the gentle evolution of Mexican trade transforming its economic narrative.

At the other end of the spectrum, you have Argentina caught in a whirlwind of economic turbulence. Working like a ship against the high tide of heavy debts and faltering international confidence, the nation often finds itself dancing an uncomfortable paso doble with global trade policies.

Wearable narratives of such trade tales weave a complex tapestry, shedding light on the intricate relationship between Latin American economics and global trade. Cuban novelist Alejo Carpentier once stated, "My literature is an exploration of reality." In our context, this reality is a captivating spectacle of Latin America's commerce narrative – a constant tango of resilience, meltdowns, recoveries, and regrowth.

This journey is not just an exploration but also an examination of how global trade policies echo across mountains of the Andes, along the Amazon River, and into the very heart of markets in bustling cities such as Buenos Aires, Santiago, and Mexico City. It is quite the saga – of evolution, power, grit, and transformation, all tied firmly to the economic realities of Latin America. So, sit back and let the tale unfurl, immerse into the dance of commerce, and, most importantly, always remember - the rhythm of trade never stops, it simply changes its beat.

Cultural Canvas

In the 'Cultural Canvas', a sub-chapter of 'Latin American Liquidity' in our journey through the book, we explore the tapestry of culture, and its profound influence on economic behaviors and policies.

Stepping into the vibrant heart of Latin America, one is immediately embraced by the profound richness of culture that permeates every facet of life, including the economic landscape. A subtle yet intricate waltz of social norms, traditional beliefs, and collective history, Latin American culture plays an intriguing role emblematic of the region's economic persona.

Amos Bronson Alcott remarked, "Who speaks to the instincts speaks to the deepest in mankind, and finds the readiest response." His words resonate profoundly as we start to interpret how each cultural thread weaves intricately into the socio-economic warp and weft of the region.

Who could forget the story of Mexico's 'Peso Crisis' of the mid-1990s? A raw display of the dichotomy between hope and despair, the crisis came as a cliffhanger to the economic novel that started with the signing of the NAFTA. It underscores how deeply embedded cultural factors can be in economic shifts. A distinct desire for independence, a cultural attribute of the Mexican people, pushed them to maintain a degree of monetary sovereignty amidst global integration, ultimately leading to an economic catastrophe.

Or the saga of the Argentine 'Corralito', when the government froze bank accounts in the country, leading to widespread protests. This didn't just emerge from poor economic planning, per se, but also a history of political instability and endemic mistrust in public institutions subtly inherited in Argentine society.

There are countless Latin American narratives that explore the complex interplay between culture and the financial sphere. Each tale not only decrypts patterns of economic behavior but also manifests the resilience and spirit of the Latin American people.

In the words of Octavio Paz, a renowned Mexican intellectual, "A tradition does not read history, it lives it." Perhaps, understanding the cultural undercurrents gives us a lucid lens to perceive the otherwise convoluted matrix of economic incidences. Delving into the 'Cultural Canvas' illuminates that finance and culture are not disjointed realms, but intertwined elements of a larger, global portrait.

By uncovering the many layers of Latin America's 'Cultural Canvas', we hope to offer you a richer understanding of its financial identity anchored in its cultural roots. The journey may be labyrinthine, but it is just as enlightening, showing us how culture drives the economic machine in ways we might never expect.

So, let us dive deep, turning the pages of economic history and culture, as we navigate through the mirage of global finance. After all, every currency has a story to tell. And behind its value, fluctuations, and trends are people, history, and, yes, culture.

Lives and Livelihoods

In 'Lives and Livelihoods', the crescendo of 'Latin American Liquidity' we turn our gaze towards the layman, exploring the intricate dance between global economic trends and the everyday lives of the Latin American citizenry. Through engaging stories and captivating personal experiences, we'll breathe life into the often faceless and impersonal world of global finance.

When we consider the financial world, we often think of stock markets, of towering glass skyscrapers, of men in suits who control the financial fate of millions. But let us not forget that at the heart of these are people, like José, a humble cacao farmer from the fertile slopes of the Andes. As currency climates shift and the markets dictate new pricings, José and millions like him are affected in myriad ways. His success or failure ultimately trickles down into the homes, schools, and storefronts of his community. Some of us may find it hard to imagine that something as distant and abstract as the foreign exchange could have an impact on the price of José's cacao beans and hence, his monthly income.

To quote Economist John Kenneth Galbraith, "Money is a singular thing. It ranks with love as man's greatest source of joy. And with death as his greatest source of anxiety." This links directly to the day-to-day lives of people like José, where lives and livelihoods are vulnerably subjected to global economic patterns that, all too often, feel out of their control.

In a small village in Mexico, the story of Maria unfolds. She owns a small store selling handmade souvenirs to tourists. A sudden increase in inflation means the cash in her hands loses its value and the economic slowdown hits the tourism industry. No tourists, no sales. Her livelihood swings on the pendulum of Latin American Liquidity. Her story is a testament to how changes in economic trends affect everyday life and society's wellbeing.

Building on Maria's anecdote, Pulitzer Prize-winning journalist, Thomas Friedman once said, "In the global economy, your worst enemy is your old boss." Which, in essence, is Maria's plight, as she is forced to react to the legacy of older, possibly outdated, economic strategies.

The stories of José and Maria represent countless others in Latin America, whose lives ebb and flow with the tides of the global economy. In this section, we begin to chart a map of these tides, connecting the dots from the fluctuations of international markets to the tangible realities experienced by regular people. It is through understanding these links, we can truly grasp the full impact of the Currency Conspiracy and the role Latin American Liquidity plays in shaping the wheels of daily life across the region.

Voices of Variety

In the realm of finance, Latin America can often feel like an enthralling cryptogram, a jigsaw puzzle full of culture, politics and gusto. Indeed, the unique financial landscape of this region is painted with strokes of volatility and value - 'Latin American Liquidity'. Among this tableau, 'Voices of Variety' shines a light on the utter diversity, bringing us tales from different walks of life to illustrate an economic reality lived and breathed by over half a billion people.

Imagine a bustling market square in Buenos Aires, a shimmering skyscraper in Sao Paulo, a lively beach café in Havana - diverse scenes from a vast continent where money, in all its forms, is the lifeblood. Let's hear their voices, hear their stories, the melodies and discords of Latin America's economic symphony.

Our first voice is Lucia, an artisan from the bustling markets of Buenos Aires. Lucia has a proverb she likes to remind her customers - "El dinero no crece en los árboles." - Money doesn't grow on trees, an age-old proverb reminding us of the value of money and hard work. Lucia's tale is one of resilience in the face of rampant inflation. Picture a woman whose creativity fuels her livelihood in an economy where prices seem to dance the tango – fast, unpredictable, passionate. Lucia's experience unravels a larger narrative about the Argentine peso's economic journey.

Cut to Guillerme, a financial analyst, staring at the dazzling skyline of Sao Paulo. He's found solace in the world of cryptocurrencies as Brazil grapples with its economic downturn. He believes in what Edmund Burke once said, "The only thing necessary for the triumph of evil is for good men to do nothing." For Guillerme, passivity towards the traditional monetary system, which he believes is marred by corruption and inefficiencies, is no longer an option.

From the sandy beaches of Havana resonates the voice of Raoul, a café owner, who navigates through the complexity of dual currencies – the Cuban Convertible Peso (CUC) and the Cuban Peso (CUP). His quote to live by is Henry Ford's, "It is well enough that people of the nation do not understand our banking and monetary system, for if they did, I believe there would be a revolution before tomorrow morning." Raoul grapples daily with the disparity between these two currencies, giving us an insight into one of the world's most unique economic systems.

These stories, these voices, present a colourful, emotional, and complex collage of economic reality. They encapsulate the diverse hardships and triumphs experienced by ordinary people navigating extraordinary circumstances. Let's listen, learn, and live through these stories, shedding light upon the global financial mirage we broadly term 'Latin American Liquidity'. After all, stories are where the statistics meet the soul.

Future Fantasies

Imagine a galleon sailing through the unknown waters of the 16th century, laden with gold and the dreams of prosperity in the New World. Now fast forward to the present day. Instead of sailing ships, we have digital innovations and economic models, but the essence remains the same - dreams of prosperity and growth, wrapped in the ornate cloak of uncertainty.

Let's begin our journey with a captivating tale, one that takes us to Argentina in the early 2000s. A nation crushed under the weight of vast debt, spiraling inflation, and a populace that had lost faith in their currency. They named it the 'Argentine Great Depression.' Yet, out of the ashes of that crisis, like a phoenix, blossomed an economy that is now one of the most influential in the region.

Argentina took a gamble - they defaulted on their debts, and in a daring manoeuvre, unpegged their currency from the United States dollar. At that moment, they embarked on the journey of economic independence. The years that followed were not easy. But this bold move helped restore faith in the Argentine Peso, and ignited a wave of nationalistic pride. It was a perhaps a real-life illustration of a quotation by the globally recognized economist John Maynard Keynes: "The difficulty lies not so much in developing new ideas as in escaping from old ones."

Their neighbor, Brazil, went down a different path. Harnessing the power of commodities and focusing on fortifying domestic growth, Brazil brought about what is widely referred to as the 'Brazilian Miracle.' Despite countless hurdles, they aggressively pursued economic diversification, empowering the underprivileged and aiming for inclusive growth. Their journey echoes the words of Mahatma Gandhi: "The future depends on what you do today."

What all these scenarios teach us is that the future is truly a mirage, a puzzle of infinite possibilities. Yet, as we traverse through this complex labyrinth, certain common threads bind these stories together - the quest for financial stability, the willingness to innovate, and the courage to take bold decisions amid uncertainty.

As we delve deeper into 'Future Fantacies,' we will unpack more anecdotal narratives from this vibrant region, painting a vivid picture of the economic future that Latin America might head towards. We will explore the influences of technology, the implications of political shifts, and the impact of global trends in shaping this dynamic economic landscape.

So come along and join us on this economic exploration, navigating the shifting sands, the twisting alleyways and the echoing chambers of the Latin American financial mirage. Let's delve into the future, basking in the luminance of possibility. As playwright George Bernard Shaw once said, "We are made wise not by the recollection of the past, but by the responsibility for our future."

OCEANIC OPERATIONS

Commodity Chorus

Thunder clouds gathered on the horizon, painting the sky with hues of impending doom. The Ocean was violent, waves high and threatening, mirroring the turmoil in the financial world today. Welcome to the sub-chapter, 'Commodity Chorus', the tapestry where commodities dance under the spotlight of Oceanic economic trends. In the mysterious aquatic vastness, there are hidden signals for the world's finance gurus.

Just as Carl Sandburg once said, "Time is the coin of your life. It is the only coin you have, and only you can determine how it will be spent", we begin this journey exploring the impact of commodities on Oceanic economies.

But first, let us begin with an anecdote involving a little island nation. For the real world, it is as distant as a forgotten dream, but for the financial analysts, this tiny Oceanic island embodied an experiment worth a thousand textbooks. Known for its massive deposits of phosphates, the island thrived on this single commodity. The nation's fiscal policy was as monochromatic as a black and white movie reel; it revolved around the phosphate reserves. But as the commodity's global impact started to wane due to emerging alternatives, the island's economy experienced more sways than a boat on a stormy night in the Pacific.

Was the island's economic turbulence purely a product of the global economic order's indifference or were there hints of a conspiracy? To cut through this mystery, we must dig deeper, penetrate the veneer of commodity transactions, and unravel the dynamic play of numbers and human behavior.

Commodities hold a conspicuous place in understanding Oceanic economic trends. They are the lifeblood of many economies in the region, dictating their ebbs and flows, their highs and lows. As author Peter Drucker declared, "The best way to predict the future is to create it". Commodity-driven economies, therefore, must navigate their own destiny, finding innovative ways to leverage their natural assets in a changing global market, avoiding the fate of our island nation.

As we dive deeper into the 'Commodity Chorus', we will explore tales of breakthroughs, witness unheard narratives of resilience, and share the wisdom of a Greek philosopher who said: "In a storm, one must be steady and know when to keep the sails full and when to take them down".

So set sail with us as we embark on this journey of discovery, through the undercurrents of commodities, riding the tsunami of change, and peering into the future with the knowledge that "In the world of economics, hope and faith coexist with great scientific pretension and also a deep desire for respectability". (John Kenneth Galbraith)

Trading Tales

In the wide-open spaces of the great southern oceans, beneath the unbroken expanse of sky, a drama of enormous magnitude is played out on a daily basis. This is the world of trade in the Oceanic region—a world where ocean waves share a subtle synchrony with economic waves, where the rhythms of the markets are as constant as the tides. As Adam Smith aptly put, "Commerce and manufactures can seldom flourish long in any state which does not enjoy a regular administration of justice, in which the people do not feel themselves secure in the possession of their property, in which the faith of contracts is not supported by law."

Indeed, in the waters and countries surrounding the Pacific and Indian Oceans, the tale of trade is a tempestuous saga, influenced by politics, hatched by policies, and driven by the dire need for economic survival and prosperity.

Have you ever wondered how the products on your supermarket shelves made their way to you? There's a story behind every jar of Vegemite, each fluffy Merino wool blanket, every elegantly bottled New Zealand Sauvignon Blanc. Every trade transaction comes with its own narrative, each stock exchange has its dream and nightmare.

Let's begin this tale with an anecdote about "the apple that turned over the cart." There once was a small, entrepreneurial Kiwi fruit grower who dreamed of selling his apples in the massive markets of Australia. These were no ordinary apples; renowned in his homeland for their crispness and unique flavor, he believed his produce could shake up the Australian apple market. However, his dream was stalled for almost a century, snagged in the web of restrictive trade policies and quarantines. The humble apple thus became a symbol of trade impacts, illustrating how policies can stall a dream, halt innovation, and impact the dynamics of the economy at large.

Before we delve deeper, let's hark back to the words of acclaimed economist John Maynard Keynes, "The important thing for Government is not to do things which individuals are doing already, and to do them a little better or a little worse; but to do those things which at present are not done at all." The tale of our Kiwi grower resonates with Keynes' words and makes us question - 'Is it the responsibility of the government to facilitate or frustrate trade?' We will explore these nuances of trade policies as we traverse through the myriad tales of Oceanic operations.

From the hurrying traders of Sydney's bustling finance district to the brilliance of Singapore's sprawling port, no economic stone will be left unturned. We will hitch a ride on the shipping boats carrying everything from Australian beef to the pearl treasures of the South Pacific. We'll delve into trade deals that changed the region's economic vista and examine the power dynamics of global trade negotiations. Every story will piece together parts of the puzzle, aiding us in our quest to understand the impact of trade behaviors on the Oceanic economies.

As we embark on this journey through trading tales, we encourage you to question, ponder, and immerse yourself in these narratives. Remember, in the world of economics, as in life, nothing happens in isolation. As the waters of the ocean connect nations, so does trade, shaping economies, steering politics, and determining a nation's global standing — a truly fascinating exploration.

So, dear reader, tighten your seatbelt as we navigate the turbulent yet exciting waters of Oceanic operations and put through the prismatic lens of trade tales. Each anecdote, each policy, and each insight we share endeavors to shed light on the intricate weaves of the global financial mirage. Welcome aboard!

Policy Parade

Now we delve into the murky depths of the world economy, a vast and complex machine driven by countless unseen gears and levers. One such lever, which frequently escapes the public eye, is the subtle yet significant influence of various fiscal and monetary policies on economic health and trends. Here, we will draw back the curtain and shine a spotlight on these often misunderstood gears that silently shape our financial landscape.

It is said that "Government's view of the economy could be summed up in a few short phrases: If it moves, tax it. If it keeps moving, regulate it. And if it stops moving, subsidize it." This candid observation, credited to Ronald Reagan, the 40th President of the United States, encapsulates the balancing act that is policy making - an act that can drastically impact a nation's economic outlook.

Consider the tale of Japan's 'lost decade', a story that unfolds like a doom-laden aria. In the early 1990s, a burst property and stock market bubble, compounded by poor policy responses, persisted into an economic slump that lasted for over a decade. High interest rates set by the central bank to deflate the bubble only dug the economy into a deeper hole, a clear testament to the potency of policy.

And yet, as we move across the Pacific, we find a contrasting anecdote in the United States, punctuating the previous tale of woe. Faced with the menace of the 2008 global financial crisis, the Federal Reserve deployed a novel approach. Cutting interest rates to near zero and unleashing a massive bond-buying program, it was a move that many economists credit with rescuing the U.S. economy from the jaws of depression. As Benjamin Franklin once remarked, "An investment in knowledge pays the best interest." Indeed, applying our understanding of economics to craft effective policies can yield significant dividends.

As we embark on this enlightening journey, I invite you to immerse yourself in the 'Policy Parade', relishing the rhythm of rules that underpin the global economic stage. We will meet policymakers wielding the scepter of economic power and trendsetters who dictate financial winds, all while swimming through the moderate and the murky tides they generate. Prepare to uncover the paradoxes, recognize the contradictions, and embrace the complexity of policies and their profound impact on our everyday lives.

Buckle up, dear reader, for we are about to depart on a grand tour of the global financial spectrum, a journey that promises to be as illuminating as it is captivating. The doors have opened, and the 'Policy Parade' begins...

Regional Rhythms

As we unravel the intricate tapestry of oceanic economic landscapes in this magnum opus, we set sail into the whirlpool of 'Regional Rhythms'. Picture yourself on a grand ship, ready to cast off into the seemingly insurmountable waves of international economics, with the ocean representing the vast scope of our endeavor. Each crest and trough in the water embodies the fluctuations in economic climates and financial tides of different regions.

"An oceanic perspective helps us understand regional economics, in the same way, understanding the ebb and flow of tides helps mariners navigate seas," as famously articulated by renowned economist, Henry Rowen. Delving into the depths of 'Regional Rhythms', our journey encompasses the fascinating ebb and flow of various regional economies plying the Pacific and Indian Oceans.

To kick-start our odyssey, let's swing open the door to our first stop - Australia, an economic powerhouse, thrumming to its own distinctive beat in the southern hemisphere. Imagine a tale where the arid Outback isn't just the backdrop for cinematic masterpieces, but a protagonist in its own story - propelling the Australian dollar to float against a sea of established currencies. The mining boom, spurred by the resilience of hardy Outback miners, fashioned an economic Nugget Rush, weaving a tale starkly distinctive from its Pacific neighbors.

Drifting northwards, we chart our course towards India, a land of myriad economic voices playing their distinct symphony. Here, the call of the marketplace isn't just a simple exchange of currency. No, it's a symphony, a confluence of culture, survival, and ambition that resonates in every rupee note and rattles the underpinnings of typical economic theories. "India's economy dances to the rhythm of its own tabla," as Amartya Sen, Nobel laureate in Economics, intriguingly observed.

On this riveting journey, we will navigate through the regional rhythms of numerous other coastal countries, each revealing its peculiar symphony. We'll interpret the profound impact when China's Dragon roars, and Indonesia's archipelago strums its unique melody, crafting a symphony of insightful understanding of the vast oceanic operation.

Deftly intertwined with proven facts and anecdotes, 'Regional Rhythms' promises to be a captivating helm, steering you through the turbulent tides of oceanic economies. The reader, akin to a seasoned sailor, will deftly dodge pitfalls, ride the prosperous winds, and understand the profound powers influencing the choppy seas of finance.

As the old sailor's adage goes, "You can't direct the wind, but you can adjust the sails." Even as the economies of the world keep fluctuating, those attuned to their varied and nuanced 'Regional Rhythms' indeed chart the course of prosperity. Let's hoist the sails, and head out for an enlightening exploration of oceanic economically distinct regions. Voyagers, ahoy!

Stories from the Sea

As the early dawn light painted the horizon, old sailor John Stevenson looked out across the endless expanse of water, his eyes reflecting deep wisdom and countless tales etched by the powerful tides of the sea. His life, much like the sea, had been marked by waves- some gentle and peaceful, others tumultuous and foreboding. Yet, each wave held a story, a narrative influenced significantly by the seemingly abstract trends of global economics.

Like many others, John's life and livelihood were woven into the intricate tapestry of the global economy, though he might not have often realized it. He was one sailor, on one boat, in one small coastal town. But the ocean linked him to the world, just as the intricate web of finances did. The whispers of far-off stock exchanges and boardrooms had a knack of reaching even the quietest corners of the sea, echoing through John's narratives and the lives of countless others.

Let me share with you a story, one that speaks volumes about the impacts of economic trends on communities — a story of John, his fellow sailors, and the coastal town of Dunwich. In this place, one could smell the salty sea breeze, mixed with the comforting aroma of fish and chips, the town's primary source of income and John's livelihood.

Prospering from the plentiful sea and a healthy demand from both local townsfolk and tourists, the fishing industry had been stable in Dunwich - until one day when the financial waves from across land brought unpredictable news. The global price of fish, unstable due to market speculation and overfishing, plummeted seemingly overnight.

John's words, laced with the wisdom of the waves, ring distinctly in my ears: "What catches you off guard in life isn't the storm you see comin'. It's the sudden calm that follows just a normal day, promising an even bigger storm. That's what these market things did to us."

The fishermen of Dunwich were suddenly thrust into murky waters, their stable income wavering like an unsteady boat. Hotels and restaurants, once teeming with patrons ready to partake in Dunwich's prized seafood, echoed with the hollow anxiety of uncertainty.

Yet, the spirit of the sea is resilient, just as the spirit of humanity is. As American author Herman Melville once said, "We cannot live only for ourselves. A thousand fibers connect us with our fellow men." The community of Dunwich rallied, focusing on developing sustainable fishing practices and investing in innovations to buffer against unpredictable market tides.

The stories from the sea, like John's, resonate with the rhythm of the global economy. They illustrate how the ebb and flow of the fiscal world can paint the daily realities of communities like Dunwich. As we navigate the complex straits of global finance, it's imperative to remember that the coordinates of our voyage don't merely echo in boardroom conference calls but also ripple in the simple narratives of everyday lives.

Each wave, each story, serves as a lighthouse illuminating the far-reaching corners of the global economic mirage, guiding us to the deeper understanding and empathy needed to foster both individual growth and collective prosperity.

Economic Echoes

"Whatever we do is merely a drop in the ocean. But if that drop were missing, the ocean would lack something." Mother Theresa's words speak volumes about the interconnected nature of our global economy. Each decision, policy, and event, no matter how small, can ripple throughout the world, stirring tides of change in unforeseen ways. Welcome to 'Economic Echoes', where we delve into the cascading effects of economic happenings on societies and uncover patterns often hidden beneath the surface.

When we think of economic policies and events, it's all too easy to view them as isolated instances — frantic pushes of a button in a seemingly chaotic stock exchange, the signing of a trade deal, or a country declaring bankruptcy. But these are not solitary moments. Instead, they're part of an elaborate dance where every step echoes around the globe, affecting economies, communities, and individual lives in ways we may not foresee. Remember the common saying, "When Wall Street sneezes, the world catches a cold"? This isn't just a catchy phrase; it's an economic reality.

In 2008, for instance, the collapse of Wall Street had far-reaching implications that were initially unimaginable. The ripples it sent around the world were not just economic but social and political too. Individuals lost jobs and homes, businesses shut down, and trust in governments dwindled. An entire generation was dubbed the "lost generation" due to their struggle in the aftermath. The echoes of these events are still felt today.

Sometimes, the ripple effects of economic policies can be even quieter, yet equally profound. Take the example of China opening its markets in the late 20th century. A decision spurred not by overnight contemplation but by years of internal strife and economic drudgery. This particular policy shift caused an industrial revolution, lifting millions out of poverty and propelling China into becoming a global economic powerhouse. Yet, on the flip side, it also led to economic displacement in other regions and a global shift in manufacturing power, drastically affecting local communities elsewhere.

As the famous economist, John Maynard Keynes, once mused, "The ideas of economists and political philosophers, both when they are right and when they are wrong, are more powerful than is commonly understood." Deeply embedded in this thought is the reality of our interconnected world, where an economic ripple in one place can become a powerful wave elsewhere.

As we navigate through 'Economic Echoes', we will unearth more tales of these ripples and resonating affects, emphasizing the importance of considering the broader picture and encouraging a deeper understanding of our shared global economy. Step into this ballet of economic ebb and flow, and discover how the dance steps taken today may resonate on shores far beyond tomorrow.

Navigating Narratives

'Navigating Narratives' plunges us into the swirling currents of the globe's monetary scene, outlining strategies and pathways to skirt perilous financial shoals. As we begin our expedition into these uncharted waters of economic challenges, I am reminded of Charles Darwin's wise words: "It is not the strongest of the species that survives, nor the most intelligent, but the one most responsive to change."

Our journey starts on a bitter winter morning in 2001, when a keen-eyed Japanese economist, Dr. Yukio Noguchi, stepped onto the bustling streets of Tokyo. The city, still reeling from the early 90's "Lost Decade," was teetering on the edge of another financial crisis. Dr. Noguchi, speaking at a crowded business forum that day, boldly projected the possibility of Tokyo hitting yet another iceberg, despite being anchored in the ostensibly calm financial sea.

His predictions were met with skepticism and even ridicule from his peers. Yet, in his steadfastly held vision, the financial waters of Japan were far from tranquil - hidden depths concealed an oncoming economic challenge. Noguchi's prediction hit the mark when in 2002, Tokyo found itself in yet another financial crisis. It turns out Dr. Noguchi had simply been navigated by the correct map, foreseeing potential threats where others chose not to look.

Our journey in 'Navigating Narratives' is designed to unravel the intricacies of the economic world, much like Dr. Noguchi's approach. It is not just about analytics and algorithms, but the discernment of subtler tides that direct global currency flow. As the renowned economic philosopher Adam Smith once noted, "The real tragedy of the poor is not their suffering but the loss of their anticipation."

Thus, in operation on this economic ocean, our compass should be equipped with foresight and anticipation. If we can maneuver our strategies to the ebbs and flows of economic indicators and real-world events, it may be possible to avoid the pernicious riptides of financial crisis that are often hidden beneath the surface of global economic waters.

By understanding these narratives and how they interconnect, we can navigate the monetary maze with better precision. The aim of walking you through these pathways is ultimately to help us all become better sailors in this vast, unpredictable ocean we call the global financial market. At the end of the day, as F. Scott Fitzgerald wisely noted, "It is not a question of who is right, but what is right, that is of importance."

So, fasten your seatbelts as we plunge headlong into these narratives, tasked with plotting a safe course through this mirage that is the global money illusion. Buckle up, for it is time to set sail and navigate our way towards inventive economic strategies and pathways. Prepare to sharpen your senses, as we chart our course through this financial journey, learning from narratives that illuminate conventional wisdom and challenge existing paradigms.

Prospects and Possibilities

In the vast expanses of our world's oceans, there are countless quests unveiling themselves. Yet, these are no quests for pirate treasure or ancient lodestones. Instead, what's emerging from the blue depths is a trove of opportunities - economic ventures, industrial breakthroughs, and potential global financial hotspots. Indeed, the oceanic economies are now ripe for exploration, leaving us standing on the precipice of a new financial epoch. Yet, what will the future of these economies look like, and what potential lies beneath their surfaces? Let's navigate these uncharted seas together.

"Ocean is more than a body of water; it's a symbol of stability and constancy, a testament to the fact that the world's richest and most diverse ecosystem can also be its most mysterious." - Paul Watson.

To start, let's dive into a tale of transformation. Imagine a remote island nation in the Pacific - let's call it Island X. A decade ago, Island X was grappling with alienation from global markets due to its geographical remoteness. The island's economy was struggling, relying heavily on fisheries and limited agriculture. Fast forward ten years, Island X has metamorphosed into a vibrant and thriving economy and is now a leading exporter of sustainable aquaculture and seaweed-based products.

The story of Island X is the story of the future. It's about harnessing the oceans' potential, not just for natural resources but for innovative practices that drive sustainable economic growth. This is not a single-island success story; it's part of a seismic shift we are likely to see in oceanic economies worldwide, a shift driven by technology, sustainability, and forward-thinking policy.

"Man cannot discover new oceans unless he has the courage to lose sight of the shore."- André Gide.

As we set sail further into the future, we are also likely to witness a sea-change in partnerships and collaborations. Between nations, between industries, and between ocean-based enterprises and traditional land-based economies. Flexible collaborations will become the mainsail driving growth in these emerging economies.

Take offshore wind power installations, for example. These are not just engineering marvels; they are the manifestation of incredible partnerships between policymakers, energy companies, and maritime industries. And these partnerships are now propelling countries like Denmark and the UK into the ranks of renewable superpowers.

Yet, the ebb and flow of the ocean can be unpredictable, and navigating the ocean's economic currents comes with its challenges. Investment, regulations, and conservation must all paddle in sync to ensure sustainable growth. For these oceanic economies to thrive, the focus must remain on creating wealth without depleting wealth - our ocean's natural wealth.

In conclusion, there's no denying the prosperity the oceanic economies promise, but there's a lot of voyage left. In the words of Franklin D. Roosevelt, "To reach a port, we must sail - sail, not tie at anchor - sail, not drift." These economies must continue to sail forward, resisting the urge to drift or remain anchored in old ways.

As we venture forth, trying to fathom the future of these economies, we must raise the anchor, loosen the sails, and chart a course guided by sustainability, innovation, and collaboration. Let's ride these waves with caution and curiosity, for there's many a pearl yet to be harvested from these oceanic depths.

DECODING THE CORPORATE CRYPT

Boardroom Battles

We all know the corporate crypt can be ruthless and exhilarating, yet the intricacies of those run-ins inside the boardrooms are far less well understood. If the corporation is an iceberg, the boardroom is the submerged part, seldom seen but steering the entire structure. With boardrooms being the epicenter of pivotal decisions, this section paints an unvarnished picture of these closed-door encounters and uncovers the strategies that shape our modern business landscape.

You've heard the old saying, "What happens in Vegas, stays in Vegas," right? Well, the same holds true, but with a twist in the corporate world: "What happens in the boardroom doesn't just stay in the boardroom, it literally shapes the world."

And honestly, who doesn't love a juicy boardroom story? They're full of vision, controversy, egos, breakthroughs...Our aim is more than just to tell these stories; it's to mine them for insights that can help you anticipate future moves and designs of the corporate realm.

One such riveting saga is of Apple in the late 90s, where power plays and personality clashes portrayed a perfect boardroom battle. The return of Steve Jobs, whom the board had previously ousted, would dramatically turn the company's fortune. Jobs' raw determination, coupled with his out-of-box strategies, thrashed all boardroom skepticism, and Apple emerged as the most valuable company in a span of a few years. This anecdote serves as an excellent reminder of the immense importance of strategic thinking and courage in the face of adversity that boardrooms necessitate.

Yet, it should be remembered that the boards aren't just battlegrounds of egos, they are also the soul and the conscience of the corporation, the keepers of its mission. Too often, we forget the words of Peter Drucker who reminded us: "Management is doing things right; leadership is doing the right things." Many battles are fought to secure not just earnings, but to steer the ship ethically and conscientiously.

In subsequent sections, we delve deeper and look closer at many such tales. We discuss the human side of corporate strategies, the power structures, the failures, the incredible comebacks, and the daily decisions that pave the path to success or demise. As we navigate through these chronicles, you'll find yourself gaining a clearer perspective of the corporate world's internal dynamics. And perhaps, you'll apply this gained wisdom in your own arena. After all, a well-strategized boardroom can change the fate of not just a company, but of the world at large.

Remember, as Jack Welch said, "There's no such thing as a perfect strategy. It's the moves you make once the game gets underway that will make all the difference. Because in the end, it's the boardroom battles that shape business". Buckle up, as we embark on this invaluable journey of dissecting boardroom battles in 'Decoding the Corporate Crypt', right here!

Strategy Showcase

As we dart deeper into the underbelly of corporate wars, we arrive at our next section, 'Strategy. Strap in as we journey through a riveting exploration of various corporate strategies employed to navigate transnational economic trends. If economies are oceans, the corporations then play the role of seasoned sailors, braving the rough seas with resilience, and most fascinatingly, with strategy.

Picture this, a game of chess. On one corner, we have the global markets, volatile and unpredictable, its controller, the invisible hand of economics. On the other corner, stand proud corporations, armed with an array of strategic weapons to counter the snowballing ambiguity and complexity of the markets. Economic economist John Maynard Keynes once mused, "In the long run, we are all dead." But in the world of corporate chess, there's no such luxury as the long run, only a series of short runs stitched together by the thread of strategical brilliance.

Let's center our spotlight onto the tech giant, Microsoft. Known for its innovation, the story behind its strategies is equally intriguing. Remember when Microsoft launched Bing in 2009? Many questioned the sanity of going against Google, the undisputed search engine champion. What played out was an insightful blend of corporate strategy, focusing not on a head-on collision but in offering an alternative perspective. Bing targeted areas where Google was not the dominant player, most notably in the integration of social media, and the rest is history. Reflecting on Microsoft's strategic initiative, it brings to mind a quote from Sun Tzu's revered classic, "The Art of War,"- "In the midst of chaos, there is also opportunity."

As we weave through the chapters of this strategy showcase, intrigued by the tales of corporate titans like Microsoft, we delve into the underlying thought process, the challenges, and the guiding principles, peering into the grey layer of the corporate world. These narratives unfold the strategic roadmap, demonstrate the adage 'where there is risk, there is opportunity,' and indicate that these corporate players are much more than economic entities. They are the visionary weavers of the global financial mirage.

Enter into the captivating world of corporate strategy, where Darwin's theory of 'Survival of the Fittest' meets Porter's art of strategy. Remember, "Strategy without tactics is the slowest route to victory. Tactics without strategy is the noise before defeat," noted Sun Tzu, the famous Chinese Military strategist. So, brace yourselves as we plunge into the ocean of strategies, surfing waves of threats and opportunities, maneuvering through global economic undercurrents, guided by the North Star of these corporate giants' strategic brilliance.

Now, ready to dive into the corporate crypt and unearth the treasure trove of strategies that have shaped our economic destiny?

Global Games

Now we're embarking on, through the intricate maze that is the world's economic system. With the everyday resource - currency - at its center, it can often resemble a complex board game, one that is global and ceaselessly in progress.

While we're accustomed to imagining nations as major players on this worldwide Monopoly board, there's another strategy piece maneuvering the squares with an equally robust impact - corporations.

Let's kick off with a tale that encapsulates our theme. Picture New York in the late 1800s. Cornelius Vanderbilt, a name that evokes awe in the realm of global economics, was fighting tooth and nail to unify the Staten Island ferry services, then operated by several smaller companies. How does this relate to our discussion? Well, what Vanderbilt achieved then was reflective of the disruptive, yet progressive influence corporations can wield on economic policies.

After consolidating the ferry services, Vanderbilt implemented standard prices and timelines, enhancing predictability for consumers. His actions echoed throughout the economy, triggering a ripple effect that reached far beyond the boundaries of Staten Island.

Vanderbilt's business antics epitomize Robert Collier's famous quote, "Success is the sum of small efforts, repeated day in and day out." Through gradual, persistent efforts, corporations mold economic policies, influencing sectors ranging from local trade to global finance.

Take, for instance, Apple and Google. In their race for smartphone supremacy, these tech titans have redefined economies, lobbying laws, and driving trends in countries halfway around the world. They're not merely selling devices;

they are shaping cultures, habits, and indeed, economies, through seemingly innocuous actions repeated time and again.

Corporations often remain largely invisible players, subtly influencing the squares they land on, changing rules, and frequently creating new ones. These entities can, at times, be an economic policy's puppeteer, pulling the strings that alter the course of global finance.

Yet this manipulative role of corporations is not without checks and balances. Remember, Google's antitrust indictment, a stark reminder of the limitations economic environments can impose on corporate giants.

Understanding the dynamics of 'Global Games' is like untying a Gordian knot. But, as GE's former CEO Jack Welch insightfully said, "Change before you have to." Stay flexible, adapt, and we can certainly decode this corporate crypt together, navigating through the financially charged labyrinth of our world.

So, fasten your seatbelts as we embark into the realm of corporations and their spectacular impact on world economics. In the pages ahead, we'll be unraveling the stories behind the outcomes, the victories and defeats in the world's most high-stake 'Global Games'.

Ethics and Entities

"Ethics and Entities" is more than just a mere meandering through the labyrinth of corporate economics; it's an odyssey across an ocean where each wave stands for a decision, carrying its unique moral weight and repercussions. Here we dive deeper into the murky waters of corporate decisions, and the ethical considerations intertwined therein.

Albert Einstein once said, "Relativity applies to physics, not ethics." Imagine you're a CEO of a multinational corporation. The decision is in your hands: do you cut the company's Carbon footprint at the expense of hundreds of jobs across your subsidiaries, or do you prioritize employment and community impact over environmental consciousness? Who authorizes us to determine what is the "lesser evil?" This, my dear readers, is the ethereal world of corporate ethics.

For our first foray into this topic, let's travel back in time to the 2008 global financial crisis - a disaster from which we are still feeling the aftershocks. Remember the infamous Lehman Brothers? Many wonder if their bankruptcy could have been avoided if ethical considerations were given due priority, rather than succumbing to the allure of immediate gains.

Ponder upon the words of Louis Brandeis, the former US Supreme Court Justice, who couldn't have put it better, "Good intentions will always be pleaded for every assumption of authority... But motives are seldom described for what they ought to be." Were Lehman's intentions good? Evidently, we cannot answer that. But we do know this: one decision based on potentially shaky ethical grounds shook the world and caused untold misery to thousands.

Ethics in corporate decisions isn't just about avoiding catastrophe, though. It's also found in everyday decisions. Think local grocery stores refusing to stock products made with child labor, or software companies declining lucrative contracts that come at the cost of infringing privacy laws. In every boardroom, ethics quietly paints the background, subtly influencing choices while not always getting its deserved acknowledgment.

Finance guru Warren Buffett puts it succinctly when he said, "It takes 20 years to build a reputation and five minutes to ruin it. If you think about that, you'll do things differently." And that is what this section aims to instigate - thinking differently. We aim to bring to the forefront ethical dilemmas that dwell in the darkness, often overlooked or ignored, but relentlessly shaping the corporate world.

Sit tight as we traverse the rough seas of ethics in corporate economics, examining real-life decisions, their moral repercussions, and their impact on you, society, and the world at large. Trust me; this is one expedition you won't want to miss. So, bring your moral compass along, and let's steer this ship into uncharted waters.

Trade Travails

When you toss a pebble into a pond, the ripple it creates is often much larger than the stone itself. The same principle applies to the world of global trade, where a single corporate action can send waves rippling outwards - impacting economies and livelihoods. Meandering through this chapter titled 'Decoding the Corporate Crypt', we dive deeper into the section 'Trade Travails', arming you with the understanding of how corporate actions echo in the far corners of our intertwined global economies.

Let's consider this anecdote. In 2001, Apple Inc. introduced a revolutionary product - the iPod. For those in the loop of technology, it was a slick little gadget that stored a plethora of songs. However, we often overlook the game-changing consequences of such an event on the global stage. iPod manufacturing created new trade links and economic dependencies between nations. Production plants sprouted in China, while raw materials were sourced from multiple countries such as Congo, Indonesia, and Brazil. America designed it; China assembled it and was sold globally - each introduction causing ripples through international economies.

Warren Buffet once said, "Only when the tide goes out do you discover who's been swimming naked". The impacts of these ripples, positive or negative, tell the tales of nations' economic prowess or vulnerabilities. For example, mineral-rich countries, heavily relying on selling raw materials, faced economic challenges when Apple chose to source their materials elsewhere. Similarly, economic prosperity shone on China, embracing manufacturing roles, while America thrived on high-paying design and development roles. Each corporate decision resulted in fluctuating tides in global trades and local economies.

Now, imagine thousands of companies just like Apple, each making decisions that ripple across the globe. Fewer regulations in one country could tilt the balance, luring corporations to set up factories or centers, affecting jobs, wage levels, and ultimately altering the economic landscape. The 'trade travails' are, thus, linked to corporate behavior, stretching across global economies and directly impacting the lives of everyday people.

The shadows of corporations have loomed large over global economies, and their actions, much like Shakespeare's Ariel, play tricks that can alter the course of nations. As we delve deeper into this section, we traverse through these trails that corporations leave, some as gentle as a summer breeze, others as tumultuous as a winter storm.

Trade might seem like a straightforward concept, a simple dance of supply on one hand and demand on the other. However, as we'll discover in 'Trade Travails', this dance is choreographed by the invisible hand of corporations whose performances profoundly echo around the globe.

"No one raindrop thinks it caused the flood,`' an old saying goes, reflecting how the tiny actions of one corporation could unleash a deluge impacting the global stage. 'Trade Travails' thus unveils the hidden script behind these actions, pulling back the curtain to reveal the actors that truly influence the ebb and flow of global trade.

Let our journey of understanding the enthralling world of corporate impacts on global trades and economies continue.

Consumer Consequences

Diving into the heart of 'Consumer Consequences', we submerge ourselves in a riveting exploration of the major corporations' decisions and their ripple effects on our lives. Close your eyes and imagine the global market as a giant sea, with corporations as colossal whales and consumers—everyday people like you and me—as an ecosystem of smaller aquatic beings, coexisting. What happens when these whales make a sudden twist and turn? We all feel the shift, don't we?

Ever since Adam Smith proclaimed the invisible hand of the market in "The Wealth of Nations," free market advocates have argued that corporations, through their pursuit of profit, inevitably help society. But do they always? And more importantly, who feels the consequences when they don't?

One of the stories that may echo in your mind is that of Enron and the devastating effect it had on its employees and consumers. Picture thousands of people losing their jobs, their savings, and their faith in a system they understood so little about. They were mere victims of decisions made higher up, in a crypt where the ordinary consumer was not invited. Warren Buffet, famously said, "You only find out who is swimming naked when the tide goes out." In Enron's case, when the tide went out, it was an alarming reality check for the entire society.

On a more contemporary note, consider our digital realm, dominated by tech giants like Apple, Amazon, and Google. Exciting as their technological marvels may be, there exists an underbelly that impacts consumers on multiple fronts. Who thought buying a book could turn into surrendering your shopping pattern, or asking for directions could reveal your whereabouts to a corporate entity? As Evgeny Morozov, a scholar of digital authoritarianism, put it, "We are asking the wrong question when we wonder whether our online data are safe. The right question is: safe from whom?"

Through the pages of this section, we aim to unearth the deep-seated traces of corporate actions within consumer worlds. We'll navigate this enthralling world together, understanding how a decision made inside a glass skyscraper can send shockwaves right into an ordinary living-room. Corporations indeed possess significant power over societies, markets, and governments. But remember what Spiderman's Uncle Ben once said, "With great power comes great responsibility." As we journey on, you'll be faced with the vital question: Do corporations wield their enormous power responsibly when consumers bear the consequences?

In this spirit, let's dive deep, navigate these corporate currents, and gain an understanding of their ebbs and flows in 'Consumer Consequences'. Prepare yourself, dear reader, for an enlightening ride into the annals of corporate history and its consequences on you, the consumer.

Forecasting the Future

As we lift the curtain on the global financial stage, we now embark on a journey into the future - a future where corporations could potentially wield greater influence over global economies than ever before. Buckle up, dear reader, because what you're about to delve into may well be the plot of tomorrow's financial headline.

The narrative of corporations influencing economies is not a new one. Recall the story of the East India Company, the first corporation to essentially birth a nation: colonized India. With its own army, governance structure, and a hefty influence on the British Crown, the East India Company was, in many ways, a precursor to the modern multinational corporation. To say that it influenced the economy of its times would be a gross understatement—it in many ways controlled it.

Now consider the likeness of today's colossal corporations; Amazon, Google, Facebook, and Alibaba; these corporations have as much power and influence as many thriving countries. Yes, you read that right. As astutely observed by World Bank economist Branko Milanovic, "Profit – an absurd amount of it – is what allows these companies to buy political power, avoid taxes, kill off competitors, and more."

But, dear reader, remember this; in every tale of power and influence, there is an undercurrent of strategy, manipulation, and often, conspiracy. Herein lies our quest—to dissect this financial mirage and reflect on possible future scenarios.

As we step into the future, where the line between corporations and governments blur, we enter into a realm of possibilities that is as fascinating as it is daunting. In this untamed new world, could corporations eventually hold the reins of global economies firm in their grasp? Could they shape new forms of diplomacy, dictate terms in international agreements, or even, brace yourselves, monetize Earth's very oxygen? It may appear like a dystopian dream, but dear reader, the blueprint for this reality already exists in the backrooms of big boardrooms.

Economist John Kenneth Galbraith once said, "The only function of economic forecasting is to make astrology look respectable." Regardless, we ought to speculate, ponder, and perhaps forewarn – all this in pursuit of discourse, in the hopes that future generations might not bear the brunt of corporate overreach.

In the following pages, we will dissect historical trends, analyze current scenarios, and speculate plausible future trajectories, together. Here we will weave stories from the past and present to predict what may lie ahead for the global economy under corporations' influence. We will look into the corporate mirror - and try to forecast the future.

So sit back, relax, let your imagination run wild with us as we forecast the future, reader. Because what we see may not just be a mirage after all - it might be the future itself!

GLOBAL THREADS

Mapping Movements

Imagine standing atop a mountain, with the entire world stretching out beneath you like a beautifully woven tapestry. From this vantage point, you can see the threads that span continents, linking distant lands and people with lines of vibrant color. Look closer, and you realize that what's holding all these threads together, what's directing their intricate dance, is the flow of money.

As economist Paul Samuelson said, "Economics is the study of how people and society choose to employ scarce resources." But beyond the dust-dry definitions lie the dynamic and ever-evolving stories of global economic patterns. Here we will delve into this captivating narrative through a series of insightful anecdotes and thought-provoking excerpts.

Picture, if you will, the tiny island nation of Kiribati. With a GDP hardly worth mentioning on a global scale, it may seem an unlikely player in the worldwide financial scene. Yet, as we'll discover, Kiribati is connected to the most robust economies of the world - USA, China, Germany - by unseen economic threads. The fluctuation of the Australian dollar, the strength of the US stock market, or even the economic impacts of a harsh winter in Europe are all felt on its shores.

To illustrate, let's zoom in on a day in the life of an I-Kiribati fisherman named Tauri. As we follow Tauri's story, you will witness how international currency exchange rates impact his everyday life, his immediate environment, and indeed, that of his compatriots. It serves to remind us of a statement by economist John Maynard Keynes: "The ideas of economists and political philosophers, both when they are right and when they are wrong, are more powerful than is commonly understood. Indeed, the world is ruled by little else."

Throughout this section, we will be figuratively cast adrift, riding the tumultuous waves of the global economy, feeling the ripples from powerful economies and understanding how they affect even the smallest communities. You'll discover how the thread that leads from Tauri's fishing boat in Kiribati stretches all the way to Wall Street, through the fishing industry, supermarkets, and even your own wallet!

We live in a world where the flutter of a butterfly's wings can cause a hurricane halfway around the globe, and 'Mapping Movements' will traverse the hurricanes of our modern economic landscape. By examining the interconnectedness of global economic trends and influences, we will come to understand the intricate and crucially important dance of our world economy.

With engaging stories, resonating quotes, and accessible language, we will explore the depth and breadth of the world's economic mechanisms. Prepare to embark on a journey of discovery, where distances shrink, and everything is surprisingly interconnected, forever reminding us of the words of Martin Luther King Jr: "We are caught in an inescapable network of mutuality, tied in a single garment of destiny. Whatever affects one directly, affects all indirectly."

Welcome to the dance of the global economy, where every movement counts, and every step echoes across the world.

Strategic Synchronicities

The crowd roared as a mélange of colors and national flags danced rhythmically in the air; a symbol of unity amidst diversity. This was not any sports event or United Nations summit. No, this was the heart of Wall Street – a bustling hive representative of the world's financial pulse – often both stirring curiosity and igniting fear in the hearts of many.

Strategic Synchronicities epitomizes an enigmatic dance where global economies delicately balance their individual interests while synchronously moving towards collective growth. British economist John Maynard Keynes had a way of distilling complex economic ideas into easily digestible truths. He once said, "The ideas of economists and political philosophers, both when they are right and when they are wrong are more powerful than is commonly understood." In our exploration of these synchronicities, we'll also see how the strategic alignments and collaborations in global economic landscapes shape our world.

Let's begin our journey by traversing back in time. Rewind to the mid-1940s, a period shrouded in the aftermath of World War II. The smell of war was still fresh, and nations were picking up the pieces, strategically aligning themselves to rebuild their economies. The formation of Bretton Woods System in 1944, a financial arrangement between the world's major economies, paved the foundation for our current global monetary order. Despite the dramatic collapse of this system in 1971, what has evolved is a multilayered construct where both conflict and cooperation coexist. Today, we inhabit this dichotomy.

To further elucidate this idea, let's consider the story of John and Emily, two recently graduated economics majors, both entering the global marketplace, albeit from opposite ends of the world. John, from a developing African nation, seeks to tap into emerging markets while Emily, from Wall Street, aims to explore traditional investment platforms. Despite their divergent paths, both their financial journeys are inherently intertwined in this intricate web of global finance, impacting and influenced by the strategic synchronicities in the process.

As Templar economist Richard N. Cooper articulated, "The global economy is not merely the sum of national economies but an increasingly interdependent system." And it's within this system that we find nations, like chess players, observing their counterparts, contemplating their next moves, and periodically realigning their strategies.

Glance over to China's Belt and Road Initiative or the trade agreements under the European Union. These are not just well-planned economic strategies; they exemplify strategic synchronicities. Every investment decision, every policy shift, every political dispute, and resolution are all cogs in the grand clockwork of the world economy.

So, key takeaway? As you navigate the turbulent waves of the global financial mirage, remember we're all in this intermingling dance of Strategic Synchronicities. As Keynes noted, "It is ideas, not vested interests, that are dangerous for good or evil." Stay tuned, and let's continue unraveling this captivating dance together, for in the next segment, we venture deeper into the realm of global financial conspiracies!

Pattern Perspectives

In the cacophony of a bustling open-air market, where colorfully dressed merchants tout their wares and eager buyers haggle over prices, one finds a microcosm of the global economy. Amid the hustle and bustle, discernible patterns begin to emerge, parallels to the constant ebb and flow of global financial tides.

Here we delve into the elusive trends in worldwide economic behaviors. This journey helps navigate through the labyrinth that is the global financial system. We ask, "Is there a grand scheme or unifying trend? Or is it all the unpredictable whims of profiteers and policy?"

Consider the economic boom of the post-World War era, oft-touted as the "Golden Age of Capitalism". Karl Marx once said, "History repeats itself, first as tragedy, second as farce". Echoes of this past prosperity resurface time and again in the economic demeanor of nations, sometimes as the soaring rhetoric of burgeoning economies, sometimes as the ironic quips of bubble economies reaching their tipping point.

One vivid anecdote that comes to mind is the striking similarity between the infamous Dutch Tulip Mania of the 17th century and the Bitcoin frenzy we've observed recently. The story of the Dutch Tulip bubble is not just a historical point of interest; it's an enlightening, if somewhat ominous, pattern. Prices of tulip bulbs escalated tremendously, only to crash spectacularly, leaving many in financial ruin. The fervor surrounding Bitcoin mirrors the same hysteria. Such patterns cast a shadow on the future of cryptocurrencies and other such speculative investing endeavors.

Yet, it's not all cautionary tales. Patterns can offer hope and forecast positive change. For instance, the once indebted nations of Southeast Asia today are rising economic tigers. Through the Asian Financial Crisis of 1997, we glean another noteworthy pattern - that of recovery and resilience. With prudent financial management and a growth-oriented policy, nations like Thailand and Indonesia bounced back, laying an encouraging blueprint for countries currently entangled in economic crisis.

In this section we decipher the hieroglyphics etched onto the monolith of global finance. As Robert Kiyosaki wisely asserted, "In school, we learn that mistakes are bad, and we are punished for making them. Yet, if you look at the way humans are designed to learn, we learn by making mistakes. We learn to walk by falling down. If we never fell down, we would never walk."

Thus, our examination of these patterns is not merely an exercise in economic history, but a call to learn from the missteps of our past and the potential they hold for a prosperous future. Join us as we peel back the layers of the global economy, revealing the intricate patterns woven deep within the tapestry of money, markets, and human endeavor.

Expert Examinations

Most of us, at some point in our lives, attempt to make sense of global finances the same way a beginner's chess player tries to make sense of chess grandmaster's game - with a lot of head-scratching and furrowed brows. It's complex, unpredictable, and often as mysterious as it is intriguing. This is where 'Expert Examinations' comes in to shine a torch in such seemingly darkened corridors of global finance.

Let's start this journey with an insightful story that very few people know about. Back in 2001, when Japan was in the throes of its significant economic downturn, famously known as the "Lost Decade", Takashi, a small-town business owner, constantly worried about his savings, which was rapidly diminishing due to the flailing economy. Against his family's advice, he sought a financial expert's opinion who convinced him to invest his savings to acquire US bonds. Many saw Takashi's move as risky and irrational. However, it was by attending to such expert advice that Takashi managed to turn his dwindling fortune around, demonstrating in the process the power of informed decision-making.

As the tale of Takashi reminds us, expert examinations often provide us with perspectives and insights that we would've possibly missed had we relied solely on our limited understanding. To quote the legendary investor Warren Buffet, "Risk comes from not knowing what you're doing." The significance of expert examinations in navigating global financial trends cannot be understated as it ensures we have the requisite knowledge to make informed decisions, thus negating unnecessary risks.

However, it's also crucial that we understand that financial experts, like all humans, cannot foresee exactly how the future would play out. They can only inform us of the possibilities and probabilities - the 'ifs' and 'buts'.

Consider the economic seismic shift of 2008, the sub-prime mortgage crisis in the United States. While few financial experts did predict a crisis, most failed to anticipate the sheer magnitude of the recession that ensued.

One such expert, Nouriel Roubini, who accurately predicted the crisis, was initially sidelined and dismissed by many in the financial realm. His warnings and persistent voice of caution made him a veritable prophet after the crisis, proving that sometimes the most valuable insights may emerge from the most unexpected quarters.

In the end, 'Expert Examinations' are more examination goggles, less crystal balls. They help us navigate the labyrinth that is global finance, guiding us through its tricky turns and blind corners. But remember, as Bernard Baruch, the well-known financier and statesman, once said, "The main purpose of the stock market is to make fools of as many men as possible." So, let's tread carefully into the mirage of global finance, making sure we have the best tools and information at our disposal.

Navigating Nuances

In the grand tapestry of global economics, every stitch bears significance. From the ebbs and flows of the stock market to the subtle undulations of exchange rates, each component interlaces in seamless synchrony, forming patterns that shape the world's financial reality. However, hidden beneath this intricate and ostensible harmony lie unseen forces and beneath-the-surface waves, the nuances of economic workings. Like a mirage, the system of finance can enthrall us with its obvious charms while skimming over profound insights that lurk beneath. As we delve into 'Navigating Nuances,' we will shine a light on these subtle elements, unraveling mysteries, debunking myths, and sharing lessons we can extract from past and present economic events.

Let's start by recalling the infamous Black Tuesday of October 29th, 1929, which triggered the Great Depression. Was it simply an over-inflated stock market bubble that burst? Or were there nuanced elements at play? Legendary economist John Maynard Keynes, who was actively observing this financial cataclysm, said, "Markets can remain irrational longer than you can remain solvent." This potent reminder demonstrates that beneath the waves of market trends lies an undercurrent of human behavior, irrationality, and sentiment - underexplored nuances that are crucial to understanding economic downturns.

Fast forward to 2008. The global financial crisis — a disheartening mess of subprime mortgages, sky-rocketing debts, and evaporating confidence, was a catastrophe. Reflecting on this episode, Nobel Laureate Paul Krugman commented, "Economists may not know much. But we know one thing very well: how and why nations fail." His words amplify that the crisis was more than financial missteps; it was about ignoring nuances. Decision-makers overlooked the growing disparities in income, the eroding quality of education, and the persistent racial segregation within communities - subtleties that fueled the financial meltdown.

These historical instances entreat us to look beyond the visible, encouraging a closer examination of the undersurface of economic trends. As we journey through this pursuit, we elucidate the subtle tools to forecast, control, and potentially avert disasters. Our voyage into the underbelly of the financial monster aims to foster an economic understanding fueled by prudence rather than hysteria, by insights rather than appearances.

To quote the great philosopher Socrates, "I am the wisest man alive, for I know one thing, and that is that I know nothing." Like Socrates, we too aim for wisdom through the pursuit of understanding. Let's leave no stone unturned as we navigate the world economy's nuances, revealing lessons that can guide us towards a more resilient financial future.

Get ready to embark on this enlightening journey. After all, understanding nuanced economic dynamics isn't just for financial analysts or economists—it's for anyone who seeks to decipher the complex global financial mirage and make informed financial decisions. Let's navigate nuances, together.

Wisdom from Whirlwinds

They say a smooth sea never made a skilled sailor. If that's the case, let's consider ourselves seasoned mariners.

The economic challenges we face act as savage storms; they shake us, they stir us, but, most importantly, they shape us. Isn't it true that it's in the heart of a whirlwind where we often find wisdom and clarity? Here, we will open the vault of wisdom garnered from navigating through these fiscal tempests.

Picture, if you will, the 2008 financial crisis. The supersonic bubble that had cast a deceptive glimmer over the world's economy burst with a shockingly deafening sound, leaving us to piece together the shattered fragments. Yet, Paul Volcker, the respected economist and former chairman of the Federal Reserve, emerged from the wreckage with anirrefutable sentiment, "The only thing useful banks have invented in 20 years is the ATM".

This quote might carry a note of cynicism, but it serves as a pivotal reminder for us; even amid chaos, it's paramount to keep a sense of perspective. Let's not forget the proverbial saying, "All that glitters is not gold". Ostensibly glittering advancements in banking led us to the threshold of the crisis; the true value was in the humble ATM - a reliable, essential service.

A memorable anecdote comes from the late 2000s when the seeds of technology were starting to weave themselves into the fabric of our society. Jason, a tech-observer from New York, had sensed an economic storm brewing. Instead of battening down the hatches, he chose to ride the whirlwind. He immersed himself in coding, understanding the ins and outs of the emerging tech world. He paid heed to the words of Albert Einstein, "In the middle of difficulty lies opportunity." Today, Jason is a successful software engineer and credits his early preparedness for his resilience during the subsequent tech layoffs during the recession.

Navigating through economic challenges isn't always about survival; it's also about adaptation and growth. It's about turning the dust thrown into your eyes by the whirlwind, into the sand to make bricks under your feet.

So, let the tumult continue. Let it spin us, toss us, and test us. For as and when the whirlwind subsides, we will emerge not just merely as survivors, but as sailors, skillfully charting the vast oceans of the global economy. After all, as Winston Churchill once said, "A pessimist sees the difficulty in every opportunity; an optimist sees the opportunity in every difficulty."

Through this whirlwind of wisdom, let's understand, let's learn, and most crucially, let's adapt. There's a whole world of economic landscapes yet to navigate. And remember, when the wind of change blows, some build walls, while others build windmills. The choice is yours. Welcome to the journey.

Illuminating Insights

Now we pull back the curtain on the grand stage of the global economy, shedding light on the shadowy corners often overlooked. We attempt to demystify complex theories, and unravel obfuscating terminologies, while offering invigorating perspectives on some of the most intriguing global economic scenarios. This endeavor is a little like peering into a kaleidoscope; each turn provides a different pattern, a unique insight—and we're about to dive right in.

First, consider this thought-provoking quote from the illustrious economist, John Maynard Keynes: "The ideas of economists and political philosophers, both when they are right and wrong, are more powerful than is commonly understood." This hammers home our chief objective: illuminating the power and influence of global economics, the very thread that is tightly woven into the fabric of our daily lives.

Let's start with an interesting anecdote. Suppose there's a rural farmer, 'John', in a little-known town in Vietnam. Intriguingly, John's livelihood is influenced not just by his farming skills or the weather conditions of Vietnam, but also by events happening thousands of miles away. Wondering how? The 2008 recession offers an explanation. This event rippled across the world, resulting in increased commodity costs worldwide. The price of John's chemical fertilizers shot up overnight, despite the fact that he was miles away from Wall Street. Sounds rather astonishing, doesn't it?

That's global economics for you. Its threads reach out, intertwining paths of different individuals across continents. It navigates through international trade treaties, exchange rates, import-export policies, and so much more—creating a mirage of domino effects that determine the livelihoods of millions.

Delving deeper, we'll meet 'Sophia', a software engineer working in Texas. Her company's stock plummets in response to Brexit negotiations—another point which perfectly highlights the reach of global economics. Sophia's retirement plan, which lies heavily on her company stocks, is suddenly not looking so safe.

The takeaway? "We all depend on the world far more than we realize", says economist Sylvia Nasar. Our task is to illuminate this dependency, to unravel its deeply complex entanglements, to review its incredulous mirages. With every turn we take, there's plenty of insightful views to share and knowledge to gain in this global economy's intricate design.

So, let us keep turning the kaleidoscope...

Crafting Courses

Imagine the world economy as a vast, complex tapestry woven with invisible threads connecting nations and economies. These threads encompass everything from the gold reserves of nations to the humble grocery store transaction. Nobel laureate economist Robert Shiller once said, "Finance is not merely about making money. It's about achieving our deep goals and protecting the fruits of our labor." This quote aptly encapsulates the essence of our journey through this subchapter.

Throughout history, we've seen the rise and fall of empires, financial meltdowns, moments of unexpected economic recoveries, and surprising innovations that have helped steady economic ships. Each story, an essential thread in the global fabric, can enlighten us on strengthening the economic landscape.

Take, for instance, the story of the tiny island nation of Singapore. Barely over 700 square kilometers, lacking in natural resources, it transformed from a colonial outpost into a thriving global hub of commerce in under a half-century. The guiding principle? Fiscal discipline, technological innovation, and relentless investment in human capital. This robust economic model presents a compelling blueprint that can be distilled and applied to other nations striving for economic stability.

On the other end of the spectrum, we have the intriguing saga of Iceland, which suffered a catastrophic financial collapse in 2008. How did a nation with a population roughly the size of St. Louis, USA, recover and thrive again? Simply put by embracing a counterintuitive approach; letting the banks fail, punishing the culprits, and focusing on social welfare. This approach delineates that sometimes the road less traveled can indeed make all the difference - an invaluable lesson for any economy facing adversity.

As we traverse these riveting stories, we'll also borrow wisdom from economic maestros. John Maynard Keynes, the renowned economist, once bounced back after a significant financial loss with encouraging optimism, "The market can stay irrational longer than you can stay solvent." The wisdom inherent in this statement encourages stakeholders to persevere amid economic turbulence.

The world's economic health hinges on the decisions individuals, companies, and governments make daily. So, as we weave through these historical lessons and noteworthy quotes, may we find the inspiration to craft better courses of action. Courses resilient enough to withstand the seismic waves of economic upheavals, ensuring a healthier global economy.

In "Crafting Courses," we don't simply recount mountainous financial triumphs and cavernous economic pitfalls— we strive to synthesise lessons from each strand of the global tapestry. Here's to unearthing treasure troves of ideas and strategies set to redefine the architecture of global economic health! Let's get started!

FORECASTING THE FINANCIAL CLIMATE

Trends and Trajectories

In an age where economics resembles a high-stakes spectator sport, 'Trends and Trajectories' takes you to the field, arming you with the insights you need to predict the next play in the game of global finance. Now our compass will navigate the ebb and flow of trends, even daring to predict economic trajectories yet unseen.

We're all familiar with the anecdote of the Dutch tulip mania of the 17th century, aren't we? It's an often repeated tale of blind speculation and exaggerated expectations where tulip bulbs prices soared before collapsing, leading to an economic crisis. Imagine, a simple tulip bulb, once held the same value as an entire estate! This forms our first lesson: understanding current trends is integral, but predicting future trajectories might be the key to economic survival and success.

As we trace the threads of history through the warp and weft of global economies, we will see patterns emerge, disassemble, and reform. One iconic example was the dot-com bubble of the 1990s, where rapid growth and speculative investments led to an eventual 'burst' just as spectacular as its rise.

In the immortal words of Sir John Templeton, a pioneer in mutual funds, "The four most dangerous words in investing are: 'this time it's different'". While the players and products may change, the rules of economic trends and trajectories remain the same. Bubbles inflate, reach their peak, and then inevitably burst, causing waves of disruptions. The key in this game is to observe and understand these patterns, recognize their indicators, and make informed predictions.

To further illustrate these complexities and intricacies, let's cross the Atlantic to Wall Street, which faced a crisis of epic proportions back in 2008. Recollect how the world watched in stunned silence as stalwart banking institutions crumbled like a pack of cards, triggering a global economic recession. There the subprime mortgage bubble had grown out of proportion, due to a speculative boom in housing prices, and when it eventually burst, it shook the world economy to its core.

While we can never control or fully predict these fascinating global trends, we can equip ourselves with knowledge and critical insights. We can understand the pulse of the finance world, and use this wisdom to make forecasts. As Robert Kiyosaki, author of 'Rich Dad, Poor Dad' said, "The future is unknown, but a somewhat predictable unknown. To look to the future we must first look back upon the past". In this sub-chapter, let your curiosity have free reign as we peer into the kaleidoscope of past economic trends, to foresee what the future might hold.

'Trends and Trajectories', dear reader, is your map through the ever-evolving labyrinth of global finance. May it help you navigate the mirage, one trend, one trajectory at a time, and emerge successful on the other side. Welcome to the expedition! It's time to set sail.

Warnings and Wisdom

In the murky labyrinth of global finance, there exists a chapter which belongs not to the glorious thrills of wealth accumulation, but rather to the invaluable lesions of foresight and precaution. 'Warnings and Wisdom,' - does it not sound a bit ominous, yet profoundly enlightening? Indeed, the title is suggestive of an immersion into an oracle's cave, a cave that exudes the scent of wisdom, and releases echoes of counsel aired from eons ago.

In essence, this section peels back the curtain on the thrilling drama of the economic world, intercepts echoes bouncing off the walls of the future and decodes their warnings with a clear and sharp mind, all the while leaving you, our reader, more enlightened and poles ahead in your understanding of the financial world.

Imagine for a moment walking down the bustling streets of 17th century Amsterdam. The air is thick with speculation and the clamor of traders engaged in buying and selling would fill your ears. Men bartered with fierce gusto around the budding tulip industry, an industry guided not by substantial worth, but by an overly inflated perception of value. This, as history very well documented, led to an economic apocalypse now famously known as the Tulip Mania.

Such stories underpin the edifice of 'Warnings and Wisdom', showcasing how easy it is to fall prey to financial mirages. Tulip Mania was the first recorded speculation bubble, and a very important lesson – that one must invest in tangible value, not speculative frenzy. As the renowned economist John Maynard Keynes once quipped, "The markets can stay irrational longer than you can stay solvent."

We'll not just be tied to the dock of the past but chart

course to more recent corridors of economic history, such as the 2008 economic downturn. The crash of esteemed financial giants gives us fair warning about the dangers of excessive risk, deregulation and over-reliance on mathematical models – a crash course in human over-confidence and system complacency.

Fittingly, as we walk you through stories buoyed by hubris and sunk by oversight, we'll share a simple but powerful quote from Warren Buffett: "Be fearful when others are greedy and be greedy when others are fearful." This translates into steering clear of herd mentality, stressing the importance of an independent, critical perspective when working in the financial realm.

So buckle up, because this exploration of 'Warnings and Wisdom' is not a gloomy doomsday proclamation. Rather, it's a fascinating look into the rearview mirror and a periscope gaze into the financial horizon. Our job is to ensure that when the rest of the world sees an illusion, you see it for what it truly is - a mirage.

Remember, the best way to forecast the financial climate of the future is to understand the tempests of the past. Let's embark on this journey of discovery and inoculate ourselves with wisdom – the most potent vaccine against future economic pandemics.

Navigating Novelties

In the globalized era that we're now maneuvering, economics is no longer a game relegated to the predictable movement of pieces on a chessboard. Instead, we find ourselves in the midst of a spirited polo match, where the ball strays in mouth-dropping arches and unpredictable trajectories. In this novel environment, gone are the days when economists could comfortably predict the course of markets by simply consulting their trusty old textbooks. Now, strange and unfamiliar economic winds often blow away those placid textbook predictions into the realm of fanciful thinking.

This section is your compass in understanding and navigating this new, somewhat treacherous economic landscape. As Lewis Carroll so eloquently put it in 'Alice in Wonderland', "It's no use going back to yesterday, because I was a different person then." In that spirit, we must evolve our strategies and adopt a flexible approach when confronting today's unprecedented economic events.

Take, for example, the sudden onset of the global pandemic. It struck like a tsunami, shattering economies and leaving millions of jobless people in its wake. Economists reached for their trusty textbooks only to realize - their solution manuals, well-equipped to handle slow-moving recessions, were outdated and ill-prepared for this swift catastrophe of such magnitude. How do we navigate such unpredictable and violent economic storms?

In our journey together, we'll explore the innovative strategies deployed by nations and businesses alike in weathering these unfamiliar crises. A key lesson we'll build on is the importance of resilience and adaptability, imbuing our strategies with an agility akin to that of a practiced polo player. Rather than trying to forecast economic booms and busts, successful strategists now focus on creating robust systems capable of withstanding economic shocks, whatever their nature.

Consider how eCommerce giants like Amazon beefed up their online infrastructure when traditional retail was crippling under lockdown restrictions. Or how digital currencies like Bitcoin took flight amidst global economic uncertainty. These extraordinary maneuvers aren't signs of clairvoyance but rather, a testament to the power of agility in turbulent waters.

As we journey through this section, you'll meet luminaries who, rather than fighting the current, have learned to ride it. They'll tell us in their own words how they embraced change, adapted to it, and most importantly, benefitted from it. In the words of Winston Churchill, "To improve is to change; to be perfect is to change often."

So buckle up, dear reader. We're about to embark on an enlightening journey that challenges old paradigms, paves the way for new perspectives, and helps us construct a sturdy financial lifeboat that will keep us afloat in the choppiest of economic waters. To navigate this new world, we must unlearn the old and welcome the uncharted with open arms and sharp, adaptable minds. After all, as Charles Darwin noted, "It is not the strongest of the species that survives, nor the most intelligent... It is the one that is the most adaptable to change."

Strategies for Survival

Survival, as life repeatedly reminds us, is not about being the fittest, quickest, or the strongest. It's about being the most adaptive— a poignant lesson that resonates even in the seemingly disjointed realm of global finance. The kind of resilience we are talking about here is not precipitated by brute power, but instead, by the nimbleness of mind, the agility of strategy, and above all, the foresight to see the unseen.

As the Chinese proverb says, "The best time to plant a tree was 20 years ago. The second-best time is now." This sums up our mission in this section titled 'Strategies for Survival'. It is an imperative call to action, inviting you to embark on a journey of preparation for the volatility and uncertainty that the global financial landscape can so often present.

Each economic hiccup in history, whether it be the Great Depression of the 1930s or the Global Financial Crisis of 2008, has taught us invaluable lessons but also left an indelible scar on global society. Their impact has rumbled through the generations, affecting livelihoods, shrinking economies, and even toppling governments. The common thread of survival through these tumultuous times has always been: those who best adapt, endure.

Such was the tale of John and Patricia, a couple from Michigan. In the gloomy dusk of 2008, when many were facing financial disaster, they chose to learn, adapt, and evolve. Having seen their 401(k) dwindle to an all-time low and their house value diminish by half, they intuitively knew they had to change tactics. Armed with literature on personal finance, a crash course on investing, and the will to claw their way back up, they not only survived the crisis but thrived in its aftermath. Their story stands as a testament to Benjamin Franklin's words: "By failing to prepare, you are preparing to fail."

The question before us now is not if another crisis would occur, but rather when and how well we are prepared to weather it. What are the strategies we should adopt? What are the tools we need to master? What are the economic indicators we should be observing?

As we delve deeper into the labyrinth of global finance in the forthcoming pages, we will answer these questions with features on risk management, diversification, forecasting, and much more. Drawing from the wisdom of industry pundits, the lessons from history, and the experiences of everyday heroes like John and Patricia - we will build our survival toolkit.

By the end of this journey, we aspire to equip you with the insights and the tools to not just survive, but thrive amidst the convolutions of the financial climate. As the Nigerian saying goes, "No matter how dark the cloud, there is always a thin, silver lining, and that is what we must look for." The survival strategies offered in this book will help you find your silver lining, whatever the financial weather may throw at you.

So buckle up and get ready, because, as the late Muhammad Ali once said, "He who is not courageous enough to take risks will accomplish nothing in life." And we're about to take a deep dive into the world of financial risk and reward! Let's turn uncertainty into opportunity, together.

Building Buffers

The dynamic world of finance often harbors unseen storm clouds, amassing on the distant horizon of our economic landscape. It's frequently unpredictable, like navigating through a thick mirage where things aren't always as they appear. In this unpredictable climate, 'Building Buffers' can be our beacon, our lighthouse, guiding us safely through the tumultuous waves of an ever-changing financial world.

As we journey through this chapter we will be traversing the uncharted paths towards building economic fortresses.

Let me sidetrack us into an anecdote to start us off: Imagine a sailor, well experienced, who knows the caprices of the sea all too well. Irrespective of his expertise, he still respects the unpredictability of his environment, always ready with his lifeboat. That, my dear readers, is the mindset we need to adopt when it comes to our financial voyage. Our economic lifeboat or buffer, if you will, stands as an essential tool amidst the tempestuous economic hurricanes.

Benjamin Franklin once said, "By failing to prepare, you are preparing to fail." It underlines the fact that preparation in any endeavor, especially the financial journey, holds the key to both survival and success.

In the world of finance, a 'Buffer' serves as a metaphorical shock absorber, a switch-backed trail down the steep mountain side of financial uncertainty. This chapter is about learning how to build that buffer, large enough to stand tall face to face with the worst financial storms, and nimble enough to pivot and adapt to changing economic landscapes.

Whenever financial crises arise - be it the dot-com bubble burst in 2000, the housing market crash of 2008, or the global health-caused financial challenge we are facing now - the people who weather those storms are not always the richest, but are invariably those who are most prepared: those who have built their buffers.

Hence, "Building Buffers" isn't merely about stashing away a reserve of liquid assets or erecting a tall wall of monetary brick and mortar. It's about structuring and diversifying your portfolio in a manner that allows it to both withstand hurricanes and harness the winds of change. It's about understanding your financial compass, following it, yet preparing for the times when it may inevitably fail you.

As we explore this path, we will encounter tales of economic vistas transformed by the creation of robust buffers. Stories that will embolden your financial endeavors and stiffen the resolve to build your safeguard against the unpredictable events life can toss our way.

Learning to build buffers is your life insurance on the open seas of the finance world. It's the difference between sinking and sailing. So, buckle up, as we embark on a critical journey to explore the many faces of financial security and resilience. In the words of boxing legend Joe Frazier, "You can map out a fight plan or a life plan, but when the action starts, it may not go the way you planned, and you're down to your reflexes. That's where the roadwork shows. If you cheated on that in the dark of the morning, you're getting found out now, under the bright lights."

Prudent Preparations

As we embark on this journey called 'Prudent Preparations' in the grander atmospheric context of 'Forecasting the Financial Climate', it's akin to predicting the weather. The sun may shine brilliantly, or the chill of an unforeseen blizzard might just be lingering over the horizon. The craft of personifying our global economy into weather patterns may seem far-fetched; however, it's not far from reality. The universal principle of flux, represented by the changing weather, underlines our economy's dynamic nature, full of climactic highs and plummeting lows, unpredictable as next week's forecaster's report.

Francis Bacon once said, "By far the best proof is experience." To truly understand these financial weathers then, let's reflect upon the anecdote of a Wall Street trader, John.

John proved himself a master of prudence. Back in 2007, when the weather was sunny on Wall Street, lucrative deals were the daily norm and everybody reveled in the economic boom's glory. However, John, a seasoned stockbroker, started noticing certain patterns. The housing prices were inflating ridiculously, beyond their inherent value.

John was reminded of his grandfather's words: "In an unchecked boom, the seeds of the bust are sown." He prepared, hedging his investments, diversifying across sectors resistant to downturns, creating strategies not for the sunny day today, but for the potential storm tomorrow.

And then, the 2008 financial crisis hit. As the economic hurricane wreaked havoc, most were unprepared, battered by the brutal winds. But John's foresight, marked by prudence, allowed him to weather the storm.

John's experience is a stark reminder of the ever-shifting clouds of our global economy and the importance of being prepared.

In the cold light of day, nobody can predict a crisis with unwavering certainty. But just as the clever squirrel stocks away acorns for winter, one can arm oneself with economic acorns, enabling us to stay resistant against unpredictable financial winter.

As George S. Clason illustrates beautifully in his book, "The Richest Man in Babylon," "Gold slippeth away from the man who invests it in businesses or purposes with which he is not familiar or which are not approved by those skilled in its keep." The key to prudent preparation then is not just about playing safe but understanding your game and planning with discernment.

In this section, we will detangle an array of potential economic scenarios. By learning from history, understanding macro trends, and reflecting on insightful anecdotes like John's, we aim to arm you with tools—economic acorns—that can help you prepare wisely, navigate through the most fluctuating climates, and secure your financial future effectively.

Because after all, as the old adage goes, "Forewarned, forearmed." Welcome, then, to the enlightening journey of 'Prudent Preparations'.

Innovative Insights

In the ever-shifting labyrinth of global finance, wisdom often appears as a fleeting mirage, trailing off into the far-off distance, a step beyond our reach. Welcome to the world's most daunting chessboard, where every move echoes with intended and unforeseen consequences.

Adam Smith, the undying colossus of economics, once opined, "Science is the great antidote to the poison of enthusiasm and superstition." Bearing this in mind, let us attempt to infuse a scientific spirt while navigating economic futures, with innovative strategies and unique viewpoints.

The urgency of this endeavor invites an anecdote that has fascinated me over the years. Albert Einstein, with his radical ideas, once found himself in a room filled with skeptical physicists. With a steaming blackboard, intricate notations, and a heaviness in the air, Albert started his presentation. The physics community, like our current financial gurus, were set in their ways and resistant to changeful thinking. Yet, Albert began to explain his then-controversial theory of relativity. The innovative viewpoint he offered was paradigm-shifting, it revolutionized our understanding of the universe in more ways than one. It's this kind of ground-breaking, mold-shattering thinking we must strive for when wrestling with our financial future.

Many might consider this a tall order. Indeed, Einstein himself once said, "I must be willing to give up what I am in order to become what I will be." To navigate the economic climate successfully requires a willingness to break free from traditional assumptions, to be open to new ways of thinking. Much like Einstein's peers had to change their perspective, we too must shift ours. The financial decisions we make today will ripple into the economic scenarios of tomorrow.

As we page through the colorful history of financial revolutions and economic collapses, a defining pattern emerges. The ones who weathered the strongest storms were those open to exploration and experimentation. They harnessed the power of innovation, not fearing to sail uncharted waters. Edward de Bono, a leading thinker in the realm of lateral thinking, said, "Creativity involves breaking out of established patterns in order to look at things in a different way." By embracing this mindset of innovation, we equip ourselves better to seize opportunities hidden within the vast, intimidating cornucopia of global finance.

In the chapters following, we'll dive deep into strategies that have proven to be game-changers, imbuing financial acumen with the daring spirit of Einstein himself. It's a journey that's equal parts challenging and illuminating. So, let's venture forth, unraveling the fabric of the economic future, discovering the innovative insights residing in its folds.

Stay tuned, for we have only just embarked on this amazing journey through the world of global finance, unearthing tales of economic pioneers and gathering valuable insights as we move along. Let's demystify this complex global mirage, transforming uncertainty into strategy, risk into reward, and culminating our voyage into the secure harbor of economic prosperity.

Safeguarding Sustainability

In the serpentine labyrinth of global finance, a treasure lies hidden – Sustainability, a holy grail that holds the promise of economic longevity and prosperity.

To kick things off, I'd like to share an anecdote. Meet, Hiroshi, a humble fisherman from the small coastal town of Shikoku, Japan. His very livelihood is the sea, and he has been casting his nets into the Pacific for over forty years. One day, observing the declining fish population, Hiroshi realized that his daily catch was dwindling. Instead of casting his net wider or fishing deeper, Hiroshi did something out of the ordinary. He started to fish less, focusing instead on retaining the sea's ecosystem to remain rich and diverse for future generations.

His approach mirrors our global economic practices. Much like Hiroshi, the world must make judicious use of its resources without jeopardizing future prospects. Sustainability, hence, emerges as the undercurrent to our survival, where short-term gains should never blind us to jeopardize our long-term potential.

One may argue, is not the hallmark of economy growth and more growth? While it's true that contemporary economic models often obsess over fiscal expansion, it's also equally critical to remember what John Stuart Mill stated - "Not what we have, but what we enjoy, constitutes our abundance."

This quote by Mill beautifully encapsulates the essence of sustainable economy. It's not about gaining more; it's about enjoying what we have without jeopardizing the ability of future generations to do the same.

As we delve further into this section, we will explore a myriad of proven strategies and innovative practices that champion sustainability, steering us away from the edge of financial ruin.

So sit tight, as we navigate the treacherous waters of the global financial mirage, armed with the principles of safeguarding sustainability, laying a robust groundwork for a resilient economic future. Together, we'll decipher the code to sustainable economic health, ensuring that even amidst rising tides, we keep our global ship sailing smoothly into the horizon.

LAST WORDS

Summary Saga

As we traverse the twisted corridors of the great labyrinth that is the world's financial system, we find ourselves at the final section, the 'Summary Saga'. In this part of our journey, we take a look back, gathering the pearls of wisdom seeped from the previous chapters, understanding the complex web of currency conspiracies, and making sense of the grand mirage of global finance.

Remember the tale of the Rothschilds from Chapter 2, 'The Invisible Puppeteers'? The secretive, influential, and remarkably adept banking family, the Rothschilds, shaped Europe's economic landscape. Just as a puppeteer manipulates strings to change a puppet's posture, their activities orchestrated the dances of currencies and banks. Much like H.G. Wells wisely stated, "Adapt or perish, now as ever, is nature's inexorable imperative." The Rothschilds too played along with and adeptly adapted to the unfolding economic drama, undoubtedly contributing to their lasting influence.

In the subsequent part of our saga, 'The Alchemist's Dream: Gold into Paper, ' we delved into the transformation of solid, tangible gold into abstract paper bills. It was an economic metamorphosis, changing not just the financial landscape but the world power dynamics. American author and humorist, Mark Twain, once quipped, "The lack of money is the root of all evil." But unbeknownst to many, the transformation of gold into paper allowed for a new kind of evil – currency manipulation.

The story of the 'Petrodollar System' introduced us to the world where oil became another currency, influencer, and player in the global drama. Just like the Middle Eastern deserts from which the oil is sourced, the resulting instability in global finances created ripples felt in every corner of the world.

In 'The Currency Wars and Economic Terrorism,' our voyage ventured into the intimidating battleground of economics where countries used their currency as weapons. A quote from Sun Tzu's 'Art of War' fittingly encapsulates this situation, "If you know the enemy and know yourself, you need not fear the result of a hundred battles." But as the narrative unfolded, it became clear that in this war, knowing the enemy was a daunting task.

Our penultimate chapter focused on the greatest illusion of them all - the 'Cryptocurrency Mirage'. It's like stepping into the 'Wild Wild West' where rules are still being shaped, alliances change frequently, and the potential for both boom and bust are high. As Jamie Dimon, CEO of J.P Morgan once said, "The blockchain is real." And as real as it may be, the mirage it creates, shrouded in a veil of obscurity, places it at the epicenter of financial fascination and fear.

Navigating this 'Global Financial Mirage' was not just about recounting tales of conspiracies & machinations. It was about revealing the interconnectedness of these invisible narratives through the lucid lens of finance. Behind every currency note, there lies a fascinating story, a complex web of connections, both evident and hidden.

As we conclude our thrilling journey through the financial labyrinth, the 'Summary Saga' serves as a reminder of these essential stories. It aims to transform confusing jargon into comprehensible realities and covert plots into visible imprints. Like it's said, "Money often costs too much," (Ralph Waldo Emerson). Here, costs involve not just the printed note, but the knowledge and vigilance required to navigate the ever-evolving economic corridors. The 'Summary Saga' illuminates this path through its intricate yet insightful story of global finance.

Future Foresights

Peering into the financial crystal ball requires courage, sprightly curiosity, and a generous helping of audacious imagination. But as the great physicist Niels Bohr once mused, "Prediction is very difficult, especially if it's about the future." Though we have to tread carefully, it does not mean we cannot dare to speculate, to imagine, and to forecast. After all, this is not a prediction or prophecies etched in stone, but rather a conversation- a series of hypothetical questions and possible answers meant to provoke thought and stimulate discussion.

One evening in 1971, President Nixon was faced with an unprecedented decision- to abolish the gold standard, thereby unlinking gold and the US dollar. Could he have foreseen then how this choice would catalyze a revolution in the global monetary system? Could he have predicted the thundering arrival of the Euro, Renminbi, or the fascinating world of cryptocurrencies that was yet to unfold?

What if we had a similar crossroads looming in our future? Perhaps, lurking close by in the shadowy realm of possibility, is a decision as transformative, as disruptive, and as revolutionary waiting for its moment in the sun.

Imagine a world where the dominance of the dollar is challenged by a global, decentralized digital currency. A world where the very foundation of our financial systems shifts from not just the physical or digital realm, but to the ethereal, uncharted territories of quantum finance. The choice to embrace this brave new world, or resist, is one we may have to make sooner than we expect.

Yet, as we stand on the precipice of tomorrow, a nugget of timeless wisdom from the world's most successful investor, Warren Buffet, echoes in the corridors of every financial institution: "Be fearful when others are greedy and greedy when others are fearful." Will this continue to hold true in a world where artificial intelligence dictates financial markets, and blockchain technology is the backbone of global finance? Or could there be novel opportunities and challenges that demand a fresh perspective?

These are the conversations we invite you to engage with in this final section. As we discuss the potential scenarios of our future financial world, heed the words of futurist Alvin Toffler, "The future always comes too fast and in the wrong order." But that should not deter us.

Instead, let us embrace the intelligent uncertainty, let us grapple with the exciting unknown, and let us look to the future with anticipation, preparation, and an flexible optimism. After all, the future is not just a destination, it's a journey, best embarked on with enlightened imagination and bold foresight.

Rallying Reforms

"Too big to fail" rings ominously familiar, doesn't it? Stemming from the cataclysmic financial crisis of 2008, this term came to embody a chilling perspective of our global financial system. As we traverse the labyrinthine intricacies of this economic mirage, we slowly unravel the tapestry of a system that pulses at the heart of our society. Now, as we turn our gazes towards the horizon, we edge onto the precipice of reform in 'Rallying Reforms'.

Much like the echoes of an igniting revolution, change within the financial sector possesses a captivating allure. A realist might tell you, "I am a great believer in luck, and I find the harder I work, the more I have of it" - a sentiment echoed by the venerable Thomas Jefferson. These words resonate with our reformist aspirations for the banking sector, laboring towards reinvention.

Over the years, numerous economic visionaries – consider the enigmatic Charlie Munger, for example - have cautioned us about the lack of sufficient regulatory safeguards. Charlie once keenly observed that "The best thing a human being can do is to help another human being know more." Imagine if we built an economic system underpinned by this ethos, a system built not on maximum profit, but mutual growth and knowledge.

Allow me to share an anecdote; a story, if you will, that beautifully contextualizes our journey down the rabbit hole of economic reform. When the 'Occupy Wall Street' movement first erupted in 2011, it was widely dismissed as an aimless, leaderless confusion of disgruntled citizens. Yet as this ragtag group persisted, they beamed a beacon highlighting the corruption and inequality that had become wired into our economic reality. The 'Occupy' movement was a spark that ignited a conversation globally about financial regulation and equitable distribution of wealth; a conversation, we must add, is far from over.

This story serves as a gentle reminder that no effort towards reform is ever wasted. If a battalion of determined citizens can seize the world's attention and drive discourse, think what well-thought-out policy recommendations can achieve?

As we begin this exploration into the world of economic reform, we must circle back to Albert Einstein's profound observation, "We cannot solve our problems with the same thinking we used when we created them." Building a more equitable financial system mandates a fundamental shift in our mindsets: from unconstrained capitalism reigning supreme to a controlled approach that marries profit with ethical business practices.

Join me, dear reader, as we embark upon this thrilling expedition, examining the global financial landscape through the lens of reforms and regulations. Now, more than ever, we must rally towards a complete reinvention of our financial system. For, as the great poet Robert Frost once wrote, "The best way out is always through." And through we must go. So, here we begin: 'Rallying Reforms'.

New Beginnings

As we pave our way through this final leg of our odyssey, the words of the influential philosopher, Friedrich Nietzsche, come to mind: "You must be ready to burn yourself in your own flame; how could you rise anew if you have not first become ashes?" This quote is particularly resonant in the context of our conversation on the financial landscape. As daunting as it may sound, sometimes we need to demystify and dismantle established structures to lay the foundation for novel and more equitable systems that benefit everyone, the affluent and the impoverished alike.

Let's consider the narrative of the small coastal town of Sakhinetipalli in India. The community was reeling under the heavy burden of unaffordable microcredits that shattered their fragile economy. It was then that a fervent group of women decided to take matters into their own hands.

They started the first-ever community bank run exclusively by women, heralding an era of financial independence and empowerment. Their collective action combined with an innovative strategy to offer affordable credit served as a beacon of light for many other impoverished communities. This story serves as a potent reminder that where there's a will, there's a transformation waiting to happen.

The tale of these brave women highlights the message that echoes on every page of our book - the potential of ethical leadership and active participation in the face of systemic financial setbacks. It reinforces the idea that we must stride forth, not just in discerning the financial mirage but also in paving the path that breaks free from it.

Former president and noted humanitarian Nelson Mandela once said, "Education is the most powerful weapon which you can use to change the world." This rings true for how we navigate this global financial mirage. Thus, let 'New Beginnings' serve as an invitation for every reader—an invitation to empower oneself with financial knowledge, to rise from despair and spark change. Most importantly, let's remain on this journey, learning, unlearning, and evolving continuously.

As this chapter closes, remember, we are the architects of this new era. The key is in our hands, the world waiting for us to turn the lock. As we stare into the eye of the global financial storm, let us ignite a flame from its ashes—a flame of collective action, innovative thinking, and ethical leadership that will guide us into a future where the financial mirage is replaced by a currency of equality, prosperity, and well-being for all.

So, let's embark on these new beginnings, because every ending marks the birth of a new journey. Yours begins here.

Directional Decisions

In the teetering world of global financial markets, one always stands by the crossroads of uncertainty, where every choice is a possible opportunity, or, conversely, the start of a downfall. They do not call it a 'financial jungle' for nothing, after all. Now, we unfurl the map, switch on the compass, and prepare to navigate through the layers of intrigue and deception, the so-called 'financial conspiracies'.

Every successful investor knows that beyond numbers and figures, beyond the jargon of financial analysts and Wall Street gurus, the simple act of decision-making is what brings victory or defeat. Not just any decision, but informed ones, layered with insights gathered through diligent homework and an understanding of the complexities underneath the financial landscape.

Let's begin with a well-known Wall Street tale, one of the most pivotal moments of the year 2008 - the collapse of Lehman Brothers. There was this sharp trader, let's call him 'Sam'. Sam was nothing short of a maestro when it came to betting on market movements. He had a knack for understanding the ebbs and flows, the pulse of the market. But it was during the uncertain days of 2008 that Sam exhibited uncanny resilience. While many succumbed to the panic and sold off their assets, Sam held firm. He stood still, gazing into the chaos, keeping faith in the market resilience. His decision, as bold as it was, mirrored the wisdom in the words of Warren Buffet, "Be fearful when others are greedy and greedy when others are fearful."

As the dust of the financial debacle settled, Sam emerged stronger, his decision had paid off. It was not a stroke of luck, but a choice entrenched in years of insights gained from navigating the financial marshland. This incident serves two important lessons. One, never let external chaos dictate your internal decision-making compass and two, one's understanding of the underlying financial conspiracies can indeed prove instrumental in steering clear of common pitfalls.

"Wall Street is the only place that people ride to work in a Rolls-Royce to get advice from people who take the subway," once quipped Warren Buffet, relaying the quintessential irony of the financial world. For those willing to look beyond the surface, there's always a shimmering iceberg of knowledge waiting to be discovered. To delve into the financial seas, one has to be equipped with the right set of skills - understanding the fineness of strategy is one such indispensable skill.

The gist of our discussion thus far emphasizes the power of insightful decisions. In a world beleaguered with heavily doctored data, precarious trends and financial twists, it's prudent to rely on a compass of knowledge, a deep understanding of the financial conspiracies, and the markets' mysterious ways to make decisions that propel us towards our financial goals.

Just remember— anyone can sail in the calm, but to navigate the financial mirage, you need the grit of an adventurer, the wisdom of a sage, and the foresight of a seasoned investor. Let's venture, then, into this exciting journey of unravelling financial conspiracies, and exploring how we can turn our understanding into informed, insightful decisions!

Engaging Efforts

While we navigate the choppy waters of the global financial sea, the lighthouse guiding our way isn't made of bricks and light, but of engagement, knowledge, and curiosity. From community leaders deciding on funding allocations to individuals saving for retirement, the global economy touches us in the most intimate ways. And so it is incumbent upon us to understand it, engage with it, and question it.

The late Steve Jobs once said, "Stay hungry. Stay foolish". He could have been talking about the mindset required to navigate the complex world of global finance - constantly thirsting for knowledge, embracing learning, and most importantly, being unafraid to question conventions.

Take Jane, an ordinary supermarket worker, for example, who felt a victim of her circumstance. She juggled bills, worried about her shrinking savings, and felt lost in the financial hullabaloo of Wall Street. Then Jane began to shift her perspective. She started educating herself, reading articles, attending free financial workshops, and engaging with finance professionals. Jane taught us that, in the face of confusion, the best compass is curiosity.

Then there were the members of the community of Overton - a quaint, quiet Midwestern town - who felt underrepresented in the national economy. They complained about being neglected, left to navigate the complicated financial ecosystem with no voice to influence the decisions that affected them directly. But a group of spirited individuals stepped up, establishing a neighborhood financial literacy program. These folks understood, as Helen Keller wisely observed, "Alone, we can do so little; together, we can do so much".

Whether Jane, the supermarket worker, or the community leaders of Overton, they showed us the need for continuous learning, active engagement, and critical questioning when dealing with the global financial mirage. The more involved they became, the more clarity they achieved!

As legendary investor Warren Buffet states, "Risk comes from not knowing what you're doing". Active engagement dispels ignorance, knowledge paves the way for power, and critical questioning shatters illusions. None of us can single-handedly control the vast mechanisms of the global economy. Yet, through engagement and learning, we can each influence it in our unique way.

So, here's to the Janes and Overtons of the world - those ordinary people in ordinary circumstances who take extraordinary steps. They embody the spirit of 'Engaging Efforts'. They reveal to us that we are all sailors navigating the Global Financial Mirage, charting our own course. It is through our collective engagement that we can influence change and foster a more inclusive, resilient, and transparent financial world.

And remember, in this journey of financial literacy, it's not about being right or wrong, but about asking the right questions. As Albert Einstein wisely quipped, "The important thing is not to stop questioning... Never lose a holy curiosity". Because it's only through engaging, learning, and questioning that we truly begin to pierce the global financial mirage.

Visionary Views

Every society, culture, and civilization has imagined its own future based on its present circumstances. Each era has carried with it its unique seeds of hope and dreams of a brighter, better world. As we stand on the threshold of an epoch, witnessing a pivotal shift in our global financial landscape, it's important to envision how we can shape our financial future.

Imagine if currency were a flameless candle, casting a steady and nourishing light for all to see, making all transactions open and transparent. Or, if money could grow like trees, not just in the hands of a select few, but in every individual's backyard, ensuring both fairness and sustainability. These are potent images, representing an idyllic future that seems tantalizingly close with the potentials of a reformed financial landscape.

Let me share a story about a small village in Pennsylvania. The community there has been experimenting with a local currency system. They trade their skills, services, and goods for a local currency, which can't be hoarded, encouraging fairness, and sustainability. They've seen their community flourish, connect, and prosper on a local level. Not only has this exercise engaged everyone in the community, but it has also instilled an encouraging sense of ownership and contribution toward their local economy. This is but a microcosm of what could unfold on a macro scale.

As billionaire philanthropist Warren Buffett has famously said, "Price is what you pay. Value is what you get.". This is what the reformation of our financial system aims to do - base currency on value. Putting faith in a paper bill might seem like an illusion, but trusting in the value of skills, knowledge, and services we provide is a tangible and durable concept. Shifting the mindset with a sense of collective responsibility can revolutionize how we perceive and use money.

Perhaps French philosopher Victor Hugo was peering into our future when he wrote: "Nothing is more powerful than an idea whose time has come." The radical idea of financial reform in our world is that time. A time for transparency, where every transaction made is seen and not hidden; for fairness, where every person gets a shot to create wealth equitably based on their value and contribution; and, resilience, where our financial system is not just about economic profit, but also ecological and social gains.

As we cast our gaze into the future, it is crucial to remember that change does not happen overnight. Just like a giant ship changing its course, the transformation of the financial landscape is a slow, steady process. But change it must, for as the golden words by John F. Kennedy resonate, "We choose to go to the moon in this decade and do the other things, not because they are easy, but because they are hard.". Similarly, we choose to dream, to strive, not because the path of financial reform is easy, but because it is necessary, because it is time.

In the end, the potency of this visionary perspective lies in proactive participation. As we navigate the financial mirage of the present, let's be willing sailors, committing to steer the ship of our global economy towards a more transparent, fair, and sustainable horizon. Now more than ever, in the visionary views of a brighter tomorrow, we find the inspiration and courage to act today.

Hopeful Horizons

If you've journeyed with me thus far, navigating through the tumultuous waves of the global financial realm, then I congratulate you. It takes courage to face the convoluted threadwork of currency conspiracies, the ghostly figures manipulating economies from behind velvet drapes. But as we stand at this brink, staring at financial abysses and zeniths, it's time to lift our chins, gaze beyond the immediate, and delve into the realm of 'Hopeful Horizons'.

Admittedly, it's seldom easy holding onto hope when the markets crash, our investments crumble, and the headlines scream doom. Yet, it is exactly in these moments that we must hold tight to the reins of resilience, allowing it to guide us through the storm. Remember the words of the enigmatic investor and philosopher, George Soros, "The worse a situation becomes, the less it takes to turn it around, the bigger the upside." It is a potent reminder that calamity can, rather paradoxically, create an immense potential for soaring returns.

Let me introduce you to an anecdote that springs from our not too distant past - the 2008 financial crisis. A catastrophic blend of failed financial institutions, crashing markets, bankrupted investors. No doubt, a grim portrait. Yet in this darkness, we witnessed the birth of Bitcoin, a trailblazing force in the world of digital currency. Embedded in its initial code, was a quote from The Times, "Chancellor on brink of second bailout for banks." Satoshi Nakamoto, its mysterious creator, introduced a beacon of hope when things were falling apart. An innovation that rose like a phoenix among the shredded financial systems of yesteryears, nudging us towards new and unexplored horizons.

Yes, the journey through economic oscillations and currency conspiracies can seem daunting. But as Helen Keller once said, "Although the world is full of suffering, it is also full of the overcoming of it." Archbishop Desmond Tutu resonates the same sentiment, "Hope is being able to see that there is light despite all of the darkness."

So, as we bring this chapter to a close, I urge you not to view the financial world through a lens tainted with cynicism or despair. Instead, boldly face the challenges presented today, understanding they are but stepping stones leading to a riveting future. In the compelling words of Thomas Edison, "I have not failed. I've just found 10,000 ways that won't work." Let us see every hindrance as an opportunity to create, innovate, and reformulate strategies that benefit not just us, but the global community at large.

Thus, we stand at the edge of these 'Hopeful Horizons', infused with knowledge, courage, and yes, a strong dose of optimism. Whether it's the mystery of Bitcoin, the advent of social investing, or the promise of emerging markets, let us welcome them with open arms, and leverage the opportunities they offer. For it is in these hopeful horizons that we will sketch our narrative, carving out paths of robust resilience and steadfast hope. Onwards to brighter horizons!

◆ ◆ ◆

END